What We Say, Who We Are

What We Say, Who We Are

Leopold Senghor, Zora Neale Hurston, and the Philosophy of Language

Parker English

LEXINGTON BOOKS

A division of
ROWMAN & LITTLEFIELD PUBLISHERS, INC.
Lanham • Boulder • New York • Toronto • Plymouth, UK

LEXINGTON BOOKS

A division of Rowman & Littlefield Publishers, Inc.
A wholly owned subsidiary of The Rowman & Littlefield Publishing Group, Inc.
4501 Forbes Boulevard, Suite 200
Lanham, MD 20706

Estover Road
Plymouth PL6 7PY
United Kingdom

Copyright © 2010 by Lexington Books

All rights reserved. No part of this publication may be reproduced, stored in a retrieval system, or transmitted in any form or by any means, electronic, mechanical, photocopying, recording, or otherwise, without the prior permission of the publisher.

British Library Cataloguing in Publication Information Available

Library of Congress Cataloging-in-Publication Data

English, Parker.
  What we say, who we are : Leopold Senghor, Zora Neale Hurston, and the philosophy of language / Parker English.
    p. cm.
  Includes bibliographical references and index.
  ISBN 978-0-7391-2651-6 (cloth : alk. paper)
  1. Senghor, Léopold Sédar, 1906–2001—Criticism and interpretation. 2. Hurston, Zora Neale—Criticism and interpretation. 3. Language and languages in literature. 4. Speech in literature. 5. Ethnology in literature. 6. Blacks—Languages. I. Title.
  PQ3989.S47Z626 2010
  841'.914—dc22   2009028933

Printed in the United States of America

∞™ The paper used in this publication meets the minimum requirements of American National Standard for Information Sciences—Permanence of Paper for Printed Library Materials, ANSI/NISO Z39.48-1992.

Contents

	Acknowledgments	vii
	Introduction	1
Chapter 1	Senghor's Discussion of "Negritude" and Hurston's Discussion of "Negro Expression"	9
Chapter 2	Performism: A View Gleaned from Senghor and from Hurston	21
Chapter 3	Performatives and Reflexivity in Light of Hurston's Ethnography and Fiction	35
Chapter 4	Exchanges of Speech	61
Chapter 5	Speech and Senses of Self in *Their Eyes Were Watching God*	87
Chapter 6	Performism in the World	111
	Works Cited	123
	Index	131
	About the Author	139

Acknowledgments

Among those friends from whom I have learned that much of how we see ourselves results from how we talk, about anything, it's a pleasure to thank in particular: Sheila Chick, Errol Cochrane, Pat Gabbert, Don Higdon, John Hindmarsh, Mike Hodges, B. Lloyd, Patricia Ryan, Nancy Steele, Martha Woodall.

It is also a pleasure to thank teachers who have been unusually inspiring: Cliff Hooker, John Lachs, Jim Leach, Robert Muehlmann.

Several suggestions regarding an earlier draft by an unnamed referee were helpful and are appreciated.

Portions of chapters 1, 2, and 3 are reprinted with kind permission of *Journal of Pragmatics*.

Quotations from *Their Eyes Were Watching God* are reprinted with permission of the publisher, Harper Collins Publishers.

Parker English
October 2009

Introduction

Four Theses

Let us develop four theses. First, Leopold Senghor's discussion of "negritude" (1948, 1963, 1970, 1971, 1987) overlaps with Zora Neale Hurston's discussion of "Negro expression" (1934a/1970) in several significant ways. In particular, both Senghor and Hurston think a speaker can attend to her utterances so as to enhance some sense of self. "Senghor's concept of negritude . . . remains the most comprehensive and coherent effort of reflection upon the African situation" (Irele, 1986: 393). "As an ethnographer and writer, she [Hurston] . . . is now considered one of the defining authors of the African American literary tradition" (Robinson, 1999: 982).

Second, let us use *performism* to label the view that attending to her speech can enhance a person's sense of self as this view is gleaned from some of the overlap between Senghor's and Hurston's discussions. Performism will incorporate insights from one of most prominent debates about J. L. Austin's (1962) analysis of illocutionary speech-acts, that between conventionalists and intentionalists. Third, discussion of the first two theses shows that Henry Louis Gates, Jr. (1988) is wrong to argue that Janie Crawford, the main character in Hurston's major work (1937/1998, an ethnographic novel entitled *Their Eyes Were Watching God*) is always afflicted with what W. E. B. Du Bois (1903/1989) describes as double-consciousness. Fourth, discussion of the first three theses shows that some of my Nigerian colleagues were right to suggest that Senghor's discussion of negritude, in particular, might be used to explain a certain type of speech under extreme conditions summarized after the following caveat.

A Caveat

In very broad terms, to be developed in the two chapters following, both Hurston and Senghor usually agree that continental and diasporic Africans have a somewhat unique way of speaking which enlivens both speech and speakers; which, in their terms, enhances "soul." At the foundation of this overlap between Senghor's and Hurston's discussions are two related claims. First, Blacks are relatively moved emotionally by a given situation because they tend to interpret it in terms of various performance-inviting "images," which is labeled an "affective attitude" by Senghor's commentator, Jean Paul Sartre (1948/1963). Second, Blacks generally feel enthusiasm for their emotions more than do Whites, in large part, because Blacks generally express their emotions more "dramatically" than do Whites, which Senghor labels "affective energy." Whereas Senghor's discussion presents a coherent outline of a certain view, Hurston's presents relatively many explanatory details for it. The overlap between the two discussions is remarkable, a view of speech as embodying or influencing various of a speaker's subjective senses of self.

On the other hand, our way of understanding racial differences has changed since Senghor and Hurston usually, not always, presented their discussions as uniquely true of people with relatively recent African roots. Now, there is widespread agreement that no significant biological difference distinguishes people typically identified as Black from those typically identified as White. Certainly, no such biological difference is uniquely correlated with any significant cultural difference. Furthermore, many people have ancestors who were typically identified as Black in addition to having ancestors who were typically identified as White.

So far as we will be concerned, then, it does not matter whether people typically identified as Black often utilize what Senghor calls negritude or what Hurston calls Negro expression. Nor does it matter whether only such people have access to such things. We address the issue here at the outset to, as Hurston might say, kill it dead as much as possible. What matters is that Senghor and Hurston have helped to identify a certain approach to speech as influencing self-awareness manifested by a significant number of people, whether typically identified as Black or not. Under this approach, a speaker enhances her sense of self by attending to her speech—in particular, to what Austin identifies as the illocutionary attitude embodied therein.

Speech before Imminently Inevitable Death

Between 1983 and 1987, it was my good fortune to teach philosophy at the University of Calabar, Nigeria. While English is the Nigerian lingua franca, Nigerian culture is dissimilar from as well as similar to American culture, the one within which I was raised. A major dissimilarity is that Nigeria is sometimes ruled by military governments, as occurred during all but my first three months there.

Several times, these governments publicly executed people who had participated in failed coup attempts. Neither I nor, with one exception so far as I know, any of my friends ever attended. Many friends, however, did watch some of the executions on television. I was struck by their reporting during subsequent discussions at the Senior Staff Club that one or several of the prisoners at a specific execution sang when approaching their stakes, and continued doing so till shot. Opinion was divided, but a sizeable majority thought such prisoners were meeting death with courage. Many thought most of the prisoners viewed themselves literally as patriots.

As it happened, the chair of Philosophy at the University of Lagos, J. I. Omoregbe, had just published a relevant article, "Two Ways of Looking at Death" (1981). Although Omoregbe focuses almost exclusively on natural rather than on imposed death, some of his remarks apply helpfully to the latter. More relevantly, he raises an issue helpful in introducing negritude and Negro expression.

Omoregbe (1981: 32) describes the first view of death as "optimistic" and as associated with Heidegger (1927/1973). Within this view, an awareness of death gives meaning to one's sense of self by emphasizing her singularity, and hence the uniqueness of her possibilities. Describing the second view of death as "pessimistic," Omoregbe (34–35) uses an idea associated with Sartre (1943/1956) to criticize the optimistic view. Death will actually destroy both one's sense of self and one's ability to develop her unique possibilities. "How can that which destroys be said to be useful in relation to that which it destroys?" (Omoregbe: 38).

Omoregbe "would tend to agree" with the optimistic view, mainly by shifting its focus away from a concern with each person's death as unique to him. Instead, Omoregbe's optimist is concerned with his death as inevitable. Omoregbe thinks an awareness of death as inevitable "prompts one to urgency of action. Realizing the inevitability of death, man tries to do all he can accomplish without delay" (38).[1] As a result, he gains "a sense of self-awareness . . . [concerning] his freedom and personal responsibility" (33). By itself, Omoregbe thinks this effect is "salutary."

The politically condemned men who sang to their deaths in Nigeria's soccer stadiums might be seen as guided by Omoregbe's optimistic view. Even if they understood death itself in the pessimistic way, "as the door opening upon the nothingness of human reality" (33), they also took advantage of the "undeniable portion of truth" within the optimistic view. This is the truth that, aware of death's inevitability, a person can deliberately choose what he sees as the best of available possibilities for his unique self. At the least, a person can sometimes deliberately choose the attitude with which he confronts imminently inevitable death, the type of choice described by Victor Frankl (1946/1985).

> We who lived in concentration camps can remember the men who walked through the huts comforting others, giving away their last piece of bread. They may have been few in number, but they offer sufficient proof that everything can be taken from a man but one thing: the last of the human freedoms—to choose one's attitude in any given set of circumstances, to choose one's own way. . . . Fundamentally, therefore, any man can, even under such circumstances, decide what shall become of him—mentally and spiritually. . . . It is this spiritual freedom—which cannot be taken away—that makes life meaningful and purposeful. (86–87)

Sartre seems to endorse Omoregbe's optimistic view of the political prisoners in his short story, "The Wall."[2] During the Spanish Civil War, Pablo is escorted from his cell to a Fascist firing squad. Through a twist of fate, he escapes death after he has deliberately gritted his teeth and pushed his hands into his pockets. Deliberately gritting teeth and pushing hands does, however, sustain his feeling "clean" (1939/1975: 14).

Our focusing on death as inevitable, imminently or not, is just one specific reason for sometimes deliberately choosing the acts which embody our attitudes. The more general reason is that, when they feel appropriate, a person's conscious choices of act-embodied attitude can helpfully enhance his sense of self in any situation at all. "The basic human spiritual act, then, is any appropriate emotional, intellectual, and physical expression of oneself" (Streng, 1982: 386), as illustrated by Bob Dylan.

> A lot of people . . . make it ["Don't Think Twice, It's All Right"] sort of a love song—slow and easy-going. But it isn't a love song. It's a statement that maybe you can say to make yourself feel better. It's as if you were talking to yourself. It's a hard song to sing. I can sing it sometimes, but I ain't that good yet. I don't carry myself yet the way that Big Joe Williams, Woody Guthrie, Leadbelly and Lightnin' Hopkins have carried themselves. I hope to be able to someday, but

they're older people. I sometimes am able to do it, but it happens, when it happens, unconsciously. You see, in time, with those older singers, music was a tool—a way to live more, a way to make themselves feel better at certain points. As for me, I can make myself feel better some times, but at other times, it's still hard to go to sleep at night. (as quoted by Hentoff, 1963)

Sartre, of course, agrees that our senses of self can be enhanced by our deliberate choices of embodied attitude even without the specter of death as imminently inevitable.

[A] mock feeling and a true feeling are almost indistinguishable; to decide that I love my mother and will remain with her [in France instead of joining the Free French invasion force in England], or to remain with her by putting on an act, amount somewhat to the same thing. In other words, the feeling is formed by the acts one performs. (Sartre, 1957: 27)

Regardless of whether or how we view death, then, there is good reason for us to choose acts so as to enhance a sense of self. Of course, consciously choosing our acts might simply enhance our awareness of some previously existing sense of self.

Issues to Be Addressed

Presumably, a person already well versed in such choices would employ one if eventually facing death as imminent. When I used this line of reasoning at the Staff Club in considering why the condemned prisoners might sing before their executions, some of my Nigerian colleagues directed me to writings by and about the so-called negritude authors, especially Senghor. This literature helpfully illuminates possible relationships between a person's current sense of self and her consciously chosen current ways of speaking. It thus invites discussion involving Western writers who likewise address these relationships.

This dual sort of focus is easily accomplished concerning Sartre—his "Black Orpheus" (1948/1963) is a prominent discussion of negritude, which we consider in chapters 1 and 2. We also address Hurston's discussion of "Negro expression" in chapters 1 and 2, which suggests its own explanation for why the condemned prisoners sang.

Every phase of Negro life is highly dramatized. No matter how joyful or how sad the case there is sufficient poise for drama. Everything is acted out.... [I]t satisfies the soul of its creator.[3] (1934a/1970: 24)

In addition, we follow the suggestions of Hill (1996), North (1994) and Plant (1995), in chapter 3, by unifying a view such as performism, gleaned from Senghor's discussion of negritude and from Hurston's discussion of Negro expression, with one of the most prominent debates about Austin's analysis of illocutionary speech-acts. This is the debate between "conventionalists" such as Searle (1969, 1989), and "intentionalists" such as Bach and Harnish (1979, 1992): does communicative success for explicit illocutionary speech-acts require their speakers' having certain "reflexive intentions"? Hurston's ethnographic folklore and her fiction help to show that each side of this debate is right in what it affirms but wrong in what it denies.

We also address performism with Nagel's (1969) related discussion of reflexivity in chapter 3. To use one of his terms, that helps to explain why people sometimes, not always, feel "embodied in" their speech. This, in turn, supports Plant's observation that Hurston "realized the transforming power of words and that through words, the individual could assume autonomy, naming and unnaming self" (78). A generalized form of this observation with relevance beyond Hurston is developed more fully in chapters 4 and 5, and is eventually applied to the condemned Nigerian prisoners' last speech in chapter 6.

Quirks within the Monograph

We begin by addressing Senghor's discussion of negritude and Hurston's discussion of Negro expression because each involves helpful observations about speech used to enhance a speaker's sense of self. Of course, we intend to be accurate and informative about Senghor's and Hurston's discussions. But we do not intend to be exegetical about these things. Nor do we intend to address the more general views either Senghor or Hurston might hold.[4] Rather, we are concerned only with a certain approach to speech as enhancing a speaker's sense of self that can be gleaned from Senghor's and from Hurston's discussions. The approach we will develop involves observations first presented by Senghor or by Hurston, but it will be considered as independently interesting in analyzing various speech-acts. Hopefully, some of the historical context for certain Africana cultural concepts will nonetheless seem unified with an important debate within Western philosophy of language.

Several of these discussions rely unusually much on quotes and notes. Most provide evidence for a claim or interpretation. This is especially relevant when addressing Senghor's and Hurston's views, since neither was ever presented in one unified and comprehensive publication. Several notes draw attention to certain ways of developing a claim, or to certain relationships in which it participates. Hopefully, the main flow of discussion is thus reasonably smooth while yet involving relevant commentary. Readers who wish to consider only an explicated summary of negritude should go directly to the last three pages of part A in chapter 1. Those who wish to consider only an explicated summary of Negro expression should go directly to the last two pages of part B in chapter 1. Most of chapter 2 addresses the background discussion from Senghor and from Hurston that is related to performism. Readers who wish to consider only a summary of performism itself should go directly to Section 6 therein.

Notes

1. Bob Dylan uses a related point about death as possibly imminent to explain his approach to song writing shortly before the Cuban Missile Crisis. "'**Hard Rain**' . . . is a desperate kind of song. . . . Every line in it . . . is actually the start of a whole song. But when I wrote it, I thought I wouldn't have enough time alive to write all those songs so I put all I could into this one" (as quoted by Hentoff, 1963).

2. Omoregbe quotes Sartre to explain that the latter's primary objection to the optimistic view of death is directed against its use when death is not imminently inevitable. When it is, we have only irony to fear from taking the optimistic view.

> It has often been said that we are in the situation of a condemned man among other condemned men who is ignorant of the day of his execution but who sees each day that his fellow prisoners are being executed. This is not quite exact. We ought rather to compare ourselves to a man condemned to death who is bravely preparing himself for the ultimate penalty, who is doing everything possible to make a good showing on the scaffold, and who meanwhile is carried away by a flu epidemic. (Omoregbe, 1981: 35, who quotes Sartre, 1943/1957: 211)

Sartre's sense of irony here is hard to understand. A brave man's courage seems undiminished regardless of whether he dies from flu or by the scaffold, regardless of whether it was acquired by his attending to the scaffold or to anything else. The more interesting issue would concern a man's ability to remain brave were he suddenly freed from incarceration as well as from disease, the issue eventually confronting Pablo in "The Wall."

3. While it is true that Hurston is a respected ethnographer, her research was conducted primarily in central and south Florida, New Orleans, Haiti, and Jamaica. It therefore cannot by itself adequately support her generalizing the results to all diasporic Africans, much less to continental Africans. Of course, there continues to be controversy about the extent to which any cultural generalization is significantly true of diasporic, continental, or all Africans. We should emphasize, again, that our discussion is not concerned with whether Hurston's, or Senghor's, cultural generalizations are more typically true of Blacks than of others. Our concern is with a view of

speech as influencing a speaker's sense of self that is gleaned from Hurston and from Senghor; and that is true of many people, both Black and not.

4. Together with 3,500 words of commentary, English and Kalumba (1996: 40–56) present excerpts from Senghor's more general discussions of African socialism, assimilation, and the homeland/nation distinction. The commentary discusses ideas contained in two-dozen works cited. Robinson (1999) and Wall (1997) summarize some of Hurston's more general ideas.

CHAPTER ONE

Senghor's Discussion of "Negritude" and Hurston's Discussion of "Negro Expression"

Part A: Senghor

1. Background for Senghor on Negritude

Senghor went to Paris in 1928 at the age of twenty-two as a brilliant young student who would eventually be elected to the presidency of independent Senegal (1960) as well as to membership in the French Academy (1984). The French in colonial Senegal had persuaded him of both his brilliance and, more than less, his social equality. The French in Paris, however, initially doubted his brilliance and equality because Senghor did not appear to be "a Black Frenchman," a person so assimilated into their culture as to exhibit very little of his native culture. The Parisians were similarly doubtful concerning Aimee Cesaire, Leon Damas, and most of the other Africana students in Paris who had otherwise viewed themselves as both culturally and historically different from one another.

Senghor concluded that Blacks actually do share at least one cultural feature of a very complex sort, and eventually followed the lead of Cesaire (1939/1969) in using "negritude" for designating it. Furthermore, Senghor concluded that this feature has value, even while agreeing that French culture has value; and he devoted considerable effort in helping to prove the point. Senghor was encouraged in this by the Harlem Renaissance, by the affirmative attention then being directed to Africa by European artists and ethnographers, and in particular by the views of many European surrealists.

> In them [African languages] words are always pregnant with images. Under their value as signs, their sense value shows through.
>
> The African image is not then an image by equation but an image by *analogy*, a surrealist image. . . . The object does not mean what it represents but what it suggests, what it creates. The Elephant is Strength, the Spider is Prudence; Horns are the Moon and the Moon is Fecundity. Every representation is an image, and the image, I repeat, is not an equation but a *symbol*, an ideogramme.[1] (Senghor, 1965/1979: 85)

Indeed, Senghor (1965/1979: 34) agrees with the surrealists that this way of understanding objects and people ignores "rigid logical categories" relatively much. The reason, according to Sartre (1948/1963: 34), is that Senghor thinks this way of understanding things can provide an unusual and valuable sense of self involving "immemorial powers of desire" at "the bottom of the soul." Even as president of Senegal from independence to his voluntary resignation in 1980, Senghor regarded this way of understanding as valuable despite the fact it sometimes goes beyond the conventional reality of discursive reason.

2. Intuitive Reason, Subjective Negritude, and Objective Negritude

For Senghor, the most significant culturally shared feature of Blacks is "intuitive reason," which he distinguishes from a more logic-based "discursive reason."

> We had been taught, by our French masters at the lycee, that . . . the only hope of salvation you could hold out to us was to *let ourselves be assimilated*. . . . Early on, we had become aware within ourselves that assimilation was a failure; we could assimilate mathematics or the French language, but we could never strip off our Black skins nor root out our Black souls. And so we set out on a fervent quest for the Holy Grail, which was our *Collective Soul*. And we came upon it. . . . That mere discursive reason, the *reason which only sees*, was inadequate to "comprehend" the world, to gather it up and transform it; that it needed the help of intuitive reason, *the reason which comes to grips*, which delves beneath the surface of facts and things. (1963: 9–11)

A significant feature of those who reason intuitively, according to Senghor (1959/1967: 49), is heightened sensitivity to physical phenomena, as he found exemplified by his fellow soldiers during World War II. Ba (1973: 74–75) puts the point thus: "The extreme sensitivity on the part of the Black man to everything that presents itself to his consciousness and senses is the distinctive trait of one who perceives the universe through sensuous participation, through a sort of physical intuition."

Like Senghor, Sartre regards as "subjective" the sort of negritude associated with this sensitivity, a more or less heightened and evolving state of consciousness evoked by the images suggested by other people and things. When expressed, especially verbally, this state can involve and enhance one's sense of self. On the other hand, Sartre regards as "objective" the sort of negritude comprising the cultural conditions responsible for a person's developing the type of intuitive reason that involves subjective negritude. When expressing their thoughts and feelings with intuitive reason, then, Africans participate in the objective negritude witnessed by other people.

Two of the elements of objective negritude are most important for Senghor.[2] One is animism, though it must be observed that there is no widespread agreement about the extent to which contemporary, literate Africans are animistic.

> We are dealing with a society based essentially on human relationships, or rather on the relationships between men and the "gods," with an animistic society, that is a society . . . making no distinction between natural and supernatural needs.[3] Here natural factors, and more especially social factors, are not objects. There are concealed behind them cosmic life-forces governing them, animating their appearances, giving them colour and rhythm, life and sense. It is this *significance* which imposes itself upon the consciousness and gives rise to emotion. . . . The African is moved not so much by the outward appearance of the object as by its profound reality, less by the *sign* than by its *sense*.[4] (Senghor, 1965/1979: 34)

A second most important feature of objective negritude for Senghor is the oral tradition, which is alive and well even for contemporary Africans who are literate.

> Speech seems to us the main instrument of thought, emotion and action. There is no thought or emotion without a verbal image, no free action without first a project in thought. This is even more true among peoples who disdained the written word. This explains the power of speech in Africa. The word, the spoken word, is the expression *par excellence* of the life-force, of being in its fullness. . . . For the human being, speech is the living and life-giving breath of man at prayer. It possesses a magical virtue, realizing the law of participation and by its intrinsic power, creating the thing named. (Senghor, 1965/1979: 84)

We should observe that the respected African anthropologist Robin Horton (1967: 207) agrees that traditional Africans regard speech as having magical power. However, Horton also thinks the magic of speech for a traditional

African is its being regarded as necessary or as helpful, not as sufficient, for producing certain technical results. Horton considers several explanations why incantations have remained entrenched as customs for traditional societies based on subsistence farming. The most immediately relevant explanation is that incantations help to focus a person's mind in ways conducive to his tasks. Chapter 4 below incorporates a naturalistic interpretation of magic from Chinese philosophy by virtue of which speech can be rather easily understood as having creative power at least with respect to a speaker's sense of self as related to some task at hand.

Senghor's View of Negritude
Senghor thinks Africans tend to view the perceived world animistically, as dependent on an unperceivable network of life-forces. On the one hand, life-forces are supposedly not always controlled by natural laws. On the other, life-forces, especially those of departed ancestors, are supposedly responsible for controlling the moral development of living humans. Thus, Senghor thinks Africans often view objects and people as composing a symbolic drama with personal meaning for each individual. Consequently, Africans are unusually sensitive to and emotional about objects, people, and the images associated with them. Sartre (1948/1963: 41) contrasts this sort of "affective attitude" with that of "the White proletariat," for whom "Nature is Matter, a passive resistance, a taciturn and inert opposition which he works with his tools. And Matter does not sing" (1948/1963: 12).

An African with an affective attitude, according to Senghor (1971: 43), tends to speak with "affective energy," with dramatic passion about the combination of her thoughts and emotions concerning some object or person and their associated images. This enhances her speech-embodied sense of self. On the one hand, speech itself involves an image with which she responds to one or more of those she already associates with what she takes to be the life-force(s) of certain objects or people as they relate to what she regards as her own life-force. On the other hand, Senghor also thinks it important for such a response to be expressed with appropriate rhythms.

> What is rhythm? It is the architecture of being, the internal dynamic which confers form, the system of waves given off toward the Other, the pure expression of the [speaker's] life-force. It is the vibrating shock, the power which through the sense seizes at the roots of our being.[5] (1965/1979: 87)

As people express their affective attitudes about some object or person with affective energy, according to Senghor, they surrender to its "profound reality," they reason about it intuitively. Senghor (1956: 104, as quoted by Kesteloot, 1974: 221) emphasizes that people who reason intuitively about a given situation feel unusually "authentic" if their rhythmically expressed images feel appropriate within a social interaction. Senghor thinks this typically involves amplification of a speaker's emotions. As observed above, he thinks expressed images thereby gain "sense."

In sum, Senghor thinks African societies share significant customs—animism and orality in particular. This is objective negritude. Many Africans therefore develop affective attitudes—enhanced sensitivity to and emotions as well as thoughts about the images they associate with objects and with other people. Often, an African then expresses herself with affective energy. As is customary in her society, that is, she is rhetorically dramatic in expressing her emotions and thoughts about another person or object. A person can thereby develop a more or less heightened and evolving state of consciousness concerning not only the images associated with other people and things but also her own sense of self, subjective negritude. A person's intuitive reason comprises her affective attitude, affective energy, and subjective negritude. Negritude per se is the combination of objective negritude and intuitive reason.[6]

Part B: Hurston

3. Hurston's View of Images and Drama within Negro Expression

Zora Neale Hurston was raised at the turn of the twentieth century in the central Florida town of Eatonville, an all-Black community of roughly three hundred people served by her father as mayor, preacher, and carpenter. With ethnographic research and with fiction, Hurston introduced these people into public discussion. Alan Lomax (1960: 12) describes *Mules and Men* (1935/1990), the more prominent of Hurston's two ethnographies, as "the most engaging, genuine, and skillfully written book in the field of folklore." Regarding *Their Eyes Were Watching God*, the most prominent of Hurston's four novels, Wall (1997a: 377) observes that "Hurston writes the oral culture brilliantly. 'Words walking without masters' [page 1 of *Their Eyes*] is an apt metaphor for both the novel's folk speech and its singular prose."

Hurston's View of Images and Drama in Speech
Just as Senghor does, Hurston thinks Black speech is much influenced by an oral tradition with three most important features: images, drama, and rhythm. This section considers images and drama; section 5 considers rhythm.

With respect to images, Hurston describes Blacks as thinking "in hieroglyphics." In particular, Blacks supposedly think about objects via images of their useful actions. Hurston also maintains the rich tropes of Black speech result because those who think hieroglyphically need "action words" to express their personal reactions to objects regarded in terms of such images. That is, the speech responding to hieroglyphic thought must itself project images with action words. It

> must add action to its tongue to make it do. So we have [such "double-descriptives" as] "chop-axe," "sitting-chair," "cook-pot" and the like because the speaker has in his mind the picture of the object in use. Action. Everything illustrated. So we can say the White man thinks in a written language and the Negro thinks in hieroglyphics. (1934/1970a: 24)

Others of Hurston's (25) illustrations indicate her thinking that adjectives, in addition to nouns and verbs, can help to form double-descriptives in Black speech, as is true of "high-tall" for example. Still other illustrations indicate that metaphors, similes, verbal nouns, double-negatives, onomatopoeias, neologisms, and hyperboles can add an appropriate form of action to speech for those who think hieroglyphically. Hurston (24–25) thinks these tropes result from "the will to adorn" speech that is regarded hieroglyphically.

> Hurston claimed the use of metaphor and simile ("Regular as pig tracks"), double-descriptives ("Kill-dead"), and verbal nouns ("Sense me into it") as "the Negro's greatest contribution to the language." These elements exemplify what Hurston called the "will to adorn." (Plant, 1995: 43)

Hurston regards the will to adorn speech as important for those who think hieroglyphically because she thinks they regard speech as performance. "Hurston's concept of African-American language as 'hieroglyphics' is a metaphorical way of describing verbal expression as performance" (Hill, 1996: xxxii).

> Every phase of Negro life is highly dramatised. No matter how joyful or how sad the case there is sufficient poise for drama. Everything is acted out.[7] Unconsciously for the most part of course.[8] . . . No little moment passes unadorned. . . . These little plays by strolling players are acted out daily in a dozen streets in a thousand cities, and no one ever mistakes the meaning. (Hurston, 1934/1970a: 24)
>   Last but not least, My People love a show. We love to act more than we love to see acting done. We love to look at them and we love to put them on. . . . We just love to dramatize. (Hurston, 1942/1996: 244)

Hurston regards dramatic speech in particular as "that which the soul lives by" (1935/1990: 2), which Hemenway (1977/1980: 173) describes as "psychic satisfaction." Plant (1995) explains such satisfaction as resulting from the power of speech to transform a speaker's sense of personal identity.

> Perhaps the most significant concept that Hurston drew from African American folk culture is that of the primacy of the spoken word to order reality as it empowers the self. . . . She realized the transforming power of words and that through words, the individual could assume autonomy, naming and unnaming self and world. . . . Who she was was possible to the extent that she could create, value, and define herself. . . . She constructed for herself a character that empowered her. (78)

Many critics agree that Hurston's own performances with hieroglyphic speech influenced her own sense of self. "Hurston, I feel, understood that she celebrated herself through her words, crafted herself, affirmed herself, and perhaps most important and most primal, *named* herself" (Holloway, 1987: 115).

4. Two Dramaturgical Concepts from Social Psychology

Without providing a great many details, Hill (xxii) suggests this view of speech as performance can be well-explicated by some of the "dramaturgical" concepts regarding performance originally introduced into social psychology by Erving Goffman (1959, 1986). Hill's suggestion is helpful at least with respect to two dramaturgical concepts of role-enactment respectively emphasized by Turner (1962/1990) and by Messinger, et al. (1962/1990).

With several caveats, Turner (86) observes that much of our everyday interactive behavior seems to involve ways of understanding our own roles as well as those of other people.[9] Turner describes a person as "externalistic" if her interactive goal is "to present the self in a fashion which will conform to the relevant other's conception of the role by which the actor seeks to be identified" (96). One does not simply advance a conventional item of speech in response to some conventional cue, for example. Rather, a person consciously focuses on such an exchange so as to evoke a certain audience-response concerning her, recognition that she enacts a certain role.[10] Turner thinks one's roles might then take on more importance for an individual than do the specific acts which compose those roles. "For example, the lie which is an expression of the role of friend is an altogether different thing from the same lie taken as a manifestation of the role of confidence man" (88).

Turner (94) notes the sense of self a person experiences from enacting organizational roles, in particular, need not be satisfying. Hurston agrees that a person's role-enactments can affect her sense of self. According to Hurston, however, Blacks typically exploit this opportunity precisely in order to "satisfy the soul of its creator." When certain roles negate this opportunity, they themselves tend to be rejected, as will be discussed further in chapter 3 below.

As well as enacting roles for other people, that is, Hurston thinks a Negro enacts them for herself. Hurston's view of Negro performance is not restricted to an externalistic interpretation. It is not restricted to thinking we act only to fulfill the conditions other people associate with certain roles, or even temporary images. Instead, Hurston's view also includes something like the "internalistic" interpretation of "role management" presented by Messinger, et al. (74). Under this view of internalism, we manage our "'projected' selves" so that we enhance a satisfying sense of self. Goffman provides the following example.

> [T]he act through which one can . . . try to fit into the situation is an act that can be styled to show that one is somewhat out of place. One enters the situation to the degree that one can demonstrate that one does not belong . . . [which] I shall call *role distance*. A shorthand is involved here: the individual is actually denying not the role but the virtual self that is implied in the role for all accepting performers. . . . [For example, a surgical intern has] a humbling position during surgery. . . . [E]laborate displays of role distance occurred. . . . He may rest himself by leaning on the patient or by putting a foot on an inverted bucket but in a manner too contrived to allow the others to feel it is a matter of mere resting. (1961/1990: 104, 103, 109)

For Hurston, we perform role-enactments internalistically when we manage verbal and non-verbal acts so that some satisfying sense of self is thereby embodied.

5. Hurston's View of Rhythm within Negro Expression

Hurston describes the "angularity" of rhythm as "[a]fter adornment [with images] the next most striking manifestation of the Negro" (1934/1970a: 26). She thinks the rhythms of Negro speech, music, and dance are distinguished in virtue of their "lack of symmetry . . . abrupt and unexpected changes" (1934/1970a: 26).

> The presence of rhythm and lack of symmetry are paradoxical, but there they are. Both are present to a marked degree. There is always rhythm, but it is the rhythm of segments. Each unit has a rhythm of its own, but when the whole is assembled it is lacking in symmetry. (1934/1970a: 26)

In particular, Hurston thinks a given juxtaposition of verbal rhythms might suffice for including various otherwise ill-fitting words into what seems a unified song or speech. This, even if the juxtaposition of those words is abrupt, unexpected, and incomplete, not unified in the way, say, those in a weather report are unified. Because Negro rhythm is angular, Hurston thinks it is "dynamic suggestion," it invites "responsive participation" by observers unusually much.

6. Hurston's View of Negro Expression Summarized
Hurston's view of Negro expression contains two primary elements, each of which is complex. We focus on verbal expressions in particular.

First, according to Hurston, Negroes think in hieroglyphics. They understand a given object via images of its useful actions. Furthermore, a person's verbal response to such understanding cannot be adequately expressed without involving the rich tropes of Black speech, which themselves project images. Nor can such a response be adequately delivered without a speaker's focusing, relatively often, on meeting certain dramatic conditions. For example, a speaker might focus externalistically on utterances she thinks other people regard as apt for identifying her in terms of certain roles or momentary images. For Hurston, however, it is more important that a speaker focus internalistically on managing her utterances so that satisfying senses of self are embodied therein. She not only delivers tropes, that is, but does so in ways which embody senses of self that are satisfying. Of course, the same utterance might be presented both externalistically and internalistically.

Second, Hurston thinks Negro speaking styles are often angular. The various parts of an enacted role often seem to end abruptly, and are joined together in ways that are unexpected. As a result of such angularity, however, Negro expression is dynamic suggestion or "compelling insinuation." On the one hand, it tends to seem incomplete, and so invites an audience to "add the picture" by which to compose its interpretation. A listener must therefore participate in the performance by "carrying out" the speaker's suggestions. On the other hand, the development of a Negro's role depends on how a listener responds to his interpretation of that role as developed so far. A listener should not only provide "a picture" which advances what otherwise seems an unfinished part of a speaker's role, that is, but also explicitly express his personal response to this picture. Only then does a speaker know how to develop her own role. According to Holloway, an exchange of this type "conveys self in an intimate spiritual sense" involving a "creative . . . level of consciousness" (87, 95).[11]

Notes

1. A single image can have several meanings for an African. Her situation is thus even more surrealistic. Thomson (1995) describes the following two meanings for the image of two crocodiles with a common stomach, so-called crossed crocodiles, perhaps the most pervasive image among the Akan of Ghana. It

> refers to the proverb *"funtum frafu denkyem frafu,"* literally, "bellies mixed up, crocodiles mixed up" (Cole and Ross, 1977: 10). The image is intended to discourage greediness and egoism [in a communal society] since no matter which crocodile eats the food it still goes to the same stomach. Alternatively, the crocodiles argue that the pleasure of tasting the food is part of its enjoyment. (148)

An African's situation can be seen as even more surrealistic in that she can associate more than one image with a given word or object. In addition to the image just described, for example, the Akan associate with crocodiles that of one eating a mudfish, an image with three meanings. First, "Only a bad crocodile harms the mudfish with which it shares the river" (McLeod, 1971: 93). Second, "If the mudfish in the stream grows fat, it does so to the advantage of the crocodile (to whom it may fall a victim at any time). *The prosperity of a servant is to the advantage of his master*" (Kyerematen, 1964: 48). Third, "'If the crocodile catches the mudfish it does not deal leniently with it,' a reference to the supreme power of both chief and state. . . . [Such] multiplicity of meanings attached to one motif is common in *abosodee* [sword] iconography, as in most Akan symbolism" (Ross, 1977: 90).

2. Observers such as Thomas (1965: 39) and Spleth (1985: 20) agree with Cesaire that the slave trade, colonialism, and racial discrimination have also been important parts of objective negritude. "Its [negritude's] common denominator is not skin color as such but the fact that we all belong in one way or another to a people who has suffered and continues to suffer, a people who is marginalized and oppressed" (1987/1995: 13).

So far as I know, however, there has been no attempt to explain how negritude might be identified in terms of these Western-focused factors. In particular, no one has tried to use them in distinguishing contemporary intuitive reason from any type that might have predated European contact. Rather, the Western-focused factors are actually used to explain why Senghor, Cesaire, and their Paris-colleagues became interested in identifying and discussing an already existing, traditional way of thinking they call intuitive reason. Let us thus concentrate on the objective factors explicitly emphasized by Senghor as leading to intuitive reason for Africans: animism and orality.

3. This means a person can satisfy her natural, physical needs only with support from supernatural entities—the "life-forces" of ancestors departed from her village, in particular. A significant distinction nonetheless remains with respect to "natural" things, which obey physical laws except when supernaturally disturbed, and "supernatural" things, which are capable of deliberately choosing to violate physical laws.

English and Kalumba (1996: 116, note 19) discuss one way in which this remaining distinction has been ignored.

4. Senghor (1965/1979: 36) refers to Placide Tempels (1945/1959) in explicating the concept of 'life-force' within animism. According to Tempels (53), Africans regard perceived objects as mere "manifestations" of more fundamental things, "life forces" or "vital forces." Tempels (61, 78–79, 88) thinks Africans regard life-forces, the independent "beings themselves" associated with perceived objects, as sentient agents who are responsible (to God, the Supreme Creator of everything) for the moral development of human beings. While life-forces normally respect natural laws, then, they need not do so when this would reward an undeserving person or punish a deserving one. Traditional Africans believe this explains, for example, why a given medicine cures malaria for one patient but not for another in otherwise similar situations. Tempels (1959/1996: 18–39) presents excerpts of the most salient parts of this view as advanced in his (1945/1959). English (1999) argues this view is best understood within a representationalistic conception of perception.

5. In general, Senghor (1970: 635) describes rhythm, "the main virtue, in fact, of [the affective energy part of] negritude," as "the movement of attraction or repulsion . . . symmetry and asymmetry, repetition or opposition." With specific regard to rhythm in speech, Senghor (1965/1979) thinks it involves strong and weak beats.

> Again, primacy of Speech. Rhythm gives it the fullness of power and transforms it into the Word. . . . Rhythm here does not arise from the alternation of long and short syllables but entirely from the alternation of stressed and unstressed syllables, strong beats and weak beats. (87–89)

So far as I know, Senghor provides no more details for his sense of rhythm than those above. It is, perhaps, noteworthy that most scholars regard "rhythm" as difficult to define. The entry on "rhythm" in *The New Grove Dictionary of Music*, for example, begins with the following observation: "There is no accurate simple definition of the term 'rhythm' (or 'rhythmics') and no consistent historical tradition to explain its significance" (London, 2001: 277).

6. We agree with Reed and Wake (1965/1979: 3) that it is not easy to summarize Senghor's view of negritude. "Because he has done most of his thinking about this concept polemically . . . it would be wrong to expect from his work a coherent and articulated theory of culture." We have addressed this situation by considering without citing many of Senghor's other writings as well as those of many commentaries. We agree with Markovitz (1969: 49) that "Senghor has maintained in his philosophy of Negritude a remarkably consistent core of values and concepts" which is grounded in the mainstream of thought about certain African issues.

7. Lewis (2006: 54) emphasizes that Senghor thinks Africans, in particular, perform works of art with many everyday acts. "[A]ccording to Senghor, the humane values taught by African art . . . are based on the unitary vision of the world and of life because, in Africa, all human activities, even the least significant everyday act, are integrated into art."

8. Since Hurston thinks the acting in these phases of life involves sufficient poise for drama no matter how joyful or sad, it is not clear why she thinks they are performed unconsciously. Perhaps she means simply that expressing personal reactions dramatically is so typical for many Blacks that they are not always conscious of switching from nondramatic to dramatic forms of expression. Laurence Olivier describes his own approach to acting in ordinary life thusly in note 2 of chapter 2.

9. This view of daily life in general is not without critics. Ryan (1978), for example, thinks everyday life is sufficiently different from theater that concepts used for understanding the latter are not helpful in understanding the former. Brissett and Edgley (1990a: 31) reject such criticism, however, by observing that "everything that is alleged to be distinctive of 'the theater' must in the last analyses be qualified as pertaining only to a certain type of theater." On the other hand, Brissett and Edgley (1990a: 33) also observe that Goffman himself "felt it useful to view human interaction *as if* it were drama, conceding that it could be a number of other things as well."

Without commenting further on this issue in general, we should stress that Hurston (1934/1970a: 24) specifically emphasizes her understanding that "every phase of Negro life is highly dramatised. . . . [S]omething that permeates his entire self . . . is drama. . . . Whatever the Negro does of his own volition he embellishes . . . [into] true works of art." Presumably, Hurston would agree that what she regards as Negro expression in particular can be helpfully addressed with dramaturgic concepts.

10. Turner recognizes that any role-enactment is continually subject to modification. A role "is a sort of ideal conception" which, typically, is only "hazily conceived" by its enactor. Thus, "in attempting from time to time to make aspects of the roles explicit he is creating and modifying roles as well as merely bringing them to light; the process is not only role-taking but *role-making*" (86).

11. As is true of Senghor's view of negritude, Hurston never uses a unified and comprehensive discussion to present her view of what she calls Negro expression. In his influential literary biography, for example, Robert Hemenway (1977/1980: 162) observes that Hurston introduces this view in an essay (1934/1970a) which is not only her "most analytical" but also "disorganized." As with Senghor's, we have addressed this situation by considering not only Hurston's own writings but also those of many uncited commentators. The goal is to be accurate, unified, and representative.

CHAPTER TWO

Performism: A View Gleaned from Senghor and from Hurston

1. Overlap between Senghor's Discussion of Negritude and Hurston's Discussion of Negro Expression

This chapter begins by summarizing some of the elements shared by Senghor's discussion of negritude and by Hurston's discussion of Negro expression. It then explicates one of those elements with concepts from theorists of professional acting. The chapter concludes by developing a view of speech as self-conscious performance that is gleaned from the discussions of Senghor and of Hurston.

Both Senghor and Hurston consider a type of speech they think is humanistic, each characterizing it many times as involving one's soul. Hemenway explains that Huston's approach in particular involves one's soul by providing "psychic satisfaction," while Plant elaborates that it does so by using speech in transforming one's sense of self.

More specifically, both Senghor and Hurston view a speaker as combining an affective attitude with affective energy so as to involve a more or less altered and evolving sense of self. Concerning affective attitudes, they agree that speakers tend to view objects in terms of images. Whereas Senghor associates these images with various proverbs, Hurston associates them with useful actions. On the other hand, Senghor and Hurston agree that, in practically every phase of life, speakers then dramatize their personal reactions to objects and images so as to enhance a sense of self—they display affective energy. Speakers typically do so by focusing internalistically, by dramatizing their reactions to objects and images so as to feel satisfied with the enhanced sense of self embodied in those dramatic expressions. Speakers might also focus externalistically by dramatizing their reactions in order to meet the conditions other people seem to associate with a certain role.

2. Senghor and Hurston Disagree about the Relevance of Animism for Speech

Hurston and Senghor nonetheless differ concerning the influence of animistic beliefs on a speaker's affective attitude and energy. Senghor focuses on speakers as unusually sensitive to other people or objects, as having affective attitudes, because he emphasizes they view the world in terms of life-forces, animistically inspired entities charged with the moral guidance of humans. For Senghor, speakers are unusually sensitive to the images associated with another person or object because they expect such images, at least sometimes, to result from the moral guidance of surrounding life-forces. Senghor likewise suggests an animistic link to a speaker's affective energy—her rhythmic speech is intended to awaken her life-force so that it interacts effectively with those of relevant objects and other people.

In contrast, Hurston simply ignores animism when explaining why speakers are unusually sensitive to other people or to objects, and to the images associated with them. While the case is certainly not definitive, on the other hand, an argument can be made that Hurston thinks animism is linked to affective energy for speakers. Most obviously, several of her observations about the characteristics of speech are illustrated with examples from religious ceremonies. For instance, Hurston (1934b/1970: 34) uses a person's "shouting" in church services to illustrate her observation that speech as an "emotional explosion, responsive to rhythm" can "drive out the individual consciousness." The observation is significant in that Hurston describes this custom as grounded in animism. "There can be little doubt that shouting is a survival of the African 'possession' by the gods" (1934/1970b: 34).

Such possession apparently reverses the type of animistic influence Senghor considers above. Rather than emphasizing that one's speech can awaken her life-force so that it interacts effectively with others, this type of animism emphasizes that one's speech can express the impact other life-forces make on her own. (Senghor recognizes this type of impact also.) Regardless, it is arguable that Hurston thinks animism is at least one source of a characteristic of what she thinks typical of African Americans: emotionally explosive speech.

Unfortunately, Hurston does not address this issue further. In particular, she does not link all emotionally explosive speech to shouting in church. Nor does she indicate that any characteristic of speech must be illustrated with religious examples. While Hurston is interested in animism,[1] then, it is not clear she thinks the dramatic speech of concern to her derives from animistic beliefs. She certainly does not think speakers are unusually sensitive to their environments because of such beliefs.

Rather, what Hurston emphasizes is simply that speakers dramatize their feelings, whether joyful or sad; and that they do so, often, in response to their images of encountered objects "in use." In addressing a view which is clearly gleaned from Hurston as well as from Senghor, then, we should detach a speaker's affective attitude and energy from that which, for Senghor, is their ontological source, animism.

3. Affective Attitudes and Professional Acting

With respect to actors who perform onstage Adler (1988), Hagen (1973, 1991), and Strasberg (1987) recommend enhancing a type of sensitivity related to that involved by a speaker's affective attitude. Their reason is that such enhanced sensitivity helps to "animate" an actor's subsequent behavior, making it more communicatively effective. Explicating this recommendation forms a large part of their "Method" approach to acting.

Along with the so-called representational (or formal) one, this approach to acting will be considered further in chapter 4. For the moment, we observe simply that Method actors "particularize" the objects they encounter. In addition to considering a situation's general significance, that is, Method actors sometimes consider what is personally agitating about some of the specific objects or people in this situation. "As a result of the agitation you will experience the action" (Adler: 48) when speaking, and so communicate more effectively. Such results typically involve an element which Adler, Hagen, and Strasberg call "affective memory," itself composed of what they call emotional memory and sense memory.

> I link "emotional memory" with the recall of a *psychological* or emotional response to an event moving in on me which produces sobbing, laughter, screaming, etc. I use the term "sense memory" in dealing with *physiological* sensations (heat, cold, hunger, pains, etc.). (Hagen, 1973: 46)

Strasberg denies that a successful result from Method acting must involve memories which exactly duplicate whatever unexperienced emotional or physical reactions we might find most appropriate to our current situation. All that Strasberg thinks required is our actual awareness of some memory at least vaguely associated with the current situation—from simple good cheer to complex angst, from small gestures to large ones. "The important thing is . . . not that what the actor deals with is an exact parallel . . . but that . . . the actor really experiences—something. Whatever the actor does is modified . . . by the nature and intensity of what is actually happening to him" (68).

Hurston and Senghor Confirm Method Theory's Use of Particularization in Daily Life

Most discussions of Method acting are addressed to actors as performing onstage. Strasberg (99), however, also thinks that everyone concerned with communicative "fulfillment . . . in their daily lives" should occasionally experiment with the techniques of Method acting.[2] Strasberg especially recommends that we evoke emotional memories in everyday situations by particularizing the objects therein, which he (124) also calls "concentration." The reason is that he thinks "the primary task" in communication is to enact some experience "whether it be psychological or physiological" (165).

Method theorists describe concentration in relatively general terms. They recommend simply that we focus on whatever is emotionally or sensually agitating about one or more of the things in a given situation. Holt (1992) explicates this recommendation with an animistic-type example in which material objects are regarded as attentive to oneself.

> Action places itself in a setting of its own, even as it looks around for its prop. Invention and discovery go hand-in-hand. The acting of inanimate objects—walls, trees, rivers, tombs, boats, doors, thorn bushes—makes this particularly apparent. There is an alternation of energy between the subjectivity of the player and the objectivity of the setting. . . . The whereness of action is charged with the energies of placement. That is what "taking place" means. As someone said after a powerful enactment of the castle at Elsinore, the outside of the walls was neutral, the inside attentive to what was going on.[3] (78)

Hurston's discussion of images for speakers is somewhat more specific than that of Method theorists. She observes that speakers focus on such objects in terms of their actions, especially their actions in use by people. Senghor's discussion is even more specific. He observes that speakers focus on such objects in terms of various proverbs associated with them. The upshot is that Hurston and Senghor provide independent evidence that Method theorists are right: our ability to communicate offstage can be enhanced by the particularization technique Method theorists call concentration.

A Challenge to Method Theory's Approach to Communication

On the other hand, some contemporary acting theorists who are prominent reject the Method approach to communication. This is true, for example of David Mamet (1999: 12): "'Emotional memory,' 'sense memory,' and the tenets of the Method back to and including Stanislavsky's trilogy [(1924/1948), (1936/1959), (1949/1969)] are a lot of hogwash."

One of Mamet's most basic reasons for rejecting Method communication is his thinking it boring. "The very act of striving to create an emotional state in oneself takes one out of the play. It is the ultimate self-consciousness, and though it may be self-consciousness in the service of an ideal, it is no less boring for that" (11). Given the success of Brando, James Dean, Robert De Niro, Robert Duvall, Dustin Hoffman, Marilyn Monroe, Jack Nicholson, Paul Newman, Al Pacino, and many others, Mamet's reason seems false for some Method actors.

Regardless, Mamet advances his own technique of concentration with respect to a given situation. What is significant about Mamet's technique is that it involves our focusing on present acts rather than on remembered emotions or sensations. "The ability to concentrate flows naturally from the ability to choose something interesting. Choose something legitimately interesting to do and concentration is not a problem" (95). In particular, Mamet recommends concentrations involving speech that is heartfelt. "What comes from the heart goes to the heart. The rest is Funny Voices" (63).

In effect, Mamet rejects speech associated with either an affective attitude or affective energy. He rejects the former insofar as it involves emotion-evoking images linked with an environing situation. Rather, Mamet focuses on speech itself. He rejects speech associated with affective energy insofar as speech is used with affective energy to enhance a speaker's sense of self. Again, Mamet focuses on speech itself, speech that is heartfelt. While this involves a speaker's sense of self as sincere while speaking, it does not do so to enhance this sense.

We agree with theorists of professional acting that concepts and techniques useful for communicating onstage can also be useful offstage. Furthermore, we assume that different people benefit from focusing on different sets of these things. The approach to speech we will eventually consider, performism, allows but does not require that speech be associated with a speaker's affective attitude. On the other hand, the type of speech of most concern to us is associated with a speaker's affective energy, her using speech at least in part to enhance some sense of self. Even if Mamet is right that this diminishes a speaker's communicative effectiveness, which is debatable, she can value it as serving herself.

Affective Energy

By virtue of her speech, Senghor thinks a speaker sometimes feels unusually "authentic." Our speech is then felt as "the vibrating shock, the power which through the sense seizes at the roots of our being." Even Mamet recognizes one can be moved by one's own speech. He recommends simply that actors who are most concerned with moving audiences treat this as secondary. "Now, will the outward-directed actor not be, now and again, 'moved'? Certainly, as will anyone in any circumstance, giving all of his or her attention to a task—but this emotion is a by-product, and a trivial by-product, of the performance of the action" (1999: 19).

Here, the sense of self that results from a focus on communicating effectively is subordinated to that focus itself as primary. This helps to explain how Mamet can also recommend, with some apparent exaggeration, that "the outward-directed actor . . . behaves with no regard to his personal state, but with all regard for the responses of his antagonists, which thrills the viewers" (13). The two ideas can be reconciled by emphasizing a speaker's regard for his personal state, heartfelt in speech, as subordinate to his primary goal of communicating effectively. While Mamet thinks we should be aware of ourselves as heartfelt by speaking in a certain manner, that is, he recommends we remain primarily focused on our speech as effectively communicating with other people.

Method theorists such as Hagen (1973) agree with Mamet that speech itself can enhance a person's sense of self.

> Actions themselves, verbal and physical, can generate strong emotions and can sometimes be as stimulating to an emotional release as any remembered inner object. . . . [T]here is a continuous feeding of the action by the sensation or emotion, and the emotion is furthered by the actions. (50)

Unlike Mamet but like Method theorists, Senghor and Hurston take advantage of this fact by recommending we attend to our senses of self when speaking. Senghor in particular stresses that speech often seems unusually well related with whatever thoughts and emotions are thereby expressed, and in this sense is delivered in the manner of prayer. Typically, Senghor thinks this occurs because one's speech literally amplifies the emotions it expresses. "Strangely enough, the Negro belongs to a world where speech spontaneously becomes rhythm as soon as a man is moved to emotion, restored to himself and his authenticity. Yes, speech then becomes a poem" (Senghor, 1956: 104, as quoted by Kesteloot, 1974: 221).

This view of affective energy is similar to Hurston's view of people as loving to act. Many of her commentators explain that Hurston thinks a person's enacting various images of herself allows her to "create, value, and define herself," and thereby "assume autonomy." Whereas Senghor emphasizes speech as simply amplifying one's emotions, then, Hurston emphasizes its amplifying a more complete sense of self, one involving what Gates (183–84) calls "self-understanding."[4]

In addition, Hurston extends Senghor's discussion of affective energy as expressed with surrealist images. She does so by treating a speaker's utterances as "dynamic suggestions" or "compelling insinuations" which "give the impression" to an audience. Specifically, such "angular" utterances are compelling because they sometimes seem "incomplete" or "unexpected," somewhat free of rigid logical categories.

This does not mean that Senghor or Hurston thinks speakers deliberately eschew consistency and relevance when speaking. It means only that a speaker sometimes emphasizes dramatic expression of the emotions evoked by whatever images seem most fully associated with a given situation for her. A speaker does this relatively much even if the images associated with her utterances themselves seem incomplete, even if they seem inconsistent with or irrelevant to one another. Listeners must then creatively interpret a speaker's role, and express their responses to such interpretations. Such responses invite a speaker's developing her role further. Thus, a speaker "is at once propelled and compelled by her own language" (Plant: 17). As a result, Hurston thinks a speaker sometimes "loses self-consciousness," which some of her commentators think "defines the search for the self." This explicates Senghor's observation that prayerfully delivered speech can juxtapose surrealist images whose development, according to Sartre, cannot be easily anticipated.[5]

4. Speech and Enhanced Senses of Self

Both Senghor and Hurston agree that speech can amplify some emotion already associated with a given object or person for a given speaker. Without focusing on speech as amplifying a previously existing feeling, Austin (1962) emphasizes that our feelings are often affected by our speech. "Saying something will often, or even normally, produce certain consequential effects upon the feelings . . . of the speaker" (101).

Interestingly, Hurston also thinks the affective energy of one's speech need not amplify any previously experienced feeling for a person whose speech, in

Plant's (179) terms, "empowers" her sense of self. Image-enacting speech felt as empowering, that is, can actually diminish previously experienced feelings. In this case, the affective energy of speech enhances a speaker's sense of self by diminishing an unwanted sense. The point is advanced as Janie Crawford considers Joe Starks, her store-owning second husband, after seventeen years of marriage devoid of playfulness and laughter.

> "Maybe he ain't nothin'," she cautioned herself, "but he is something in my mouth. He's got tuh be else Ah ain't got nothin' tuh live for. Ah'll lie and say he is. If Ah don't, life won't be nothin' but uh store and uh house." (Hurston, 1937/1998: 76)

As a result of lying thus, Janie feels drugged into indifference regarding Joe.

> "It was like a drug. In a way it was good because it reconciled her to things. She got so she received all things with the stolidness of the earth which soaks up urine and perfume with the same indifference." (77)

Here, Janie's previously existing feeling of disappointment is replaced by indifference because of her speech, her enervating drug, her lies. Hurston thinks speech can literally diminish the way we feel even if, in some sense, we know such speech to be false. (In chapter 5, we discuss Gates's (1988) using Du Bois's (1903/1989) well-known concept of double-consciousness to explicate this claim.) Speech can do this even though, when used differently, it can amplify the way we feel. In each case, a speaker as subject of conscious experience can feel unusually unified with herself as embodied in speech that seems relatively satisfying. In each case, her felt senses of self can be constructed internalistically, in a relatively satisfying way.

Misuses of Affective Energy
Hurston (1937/1998: 1) describes those who speak with Negro expression as being "lords of sounds" who can, for example, make "burning statements with questions." For Hemenway (1977/1980: 195), this "adds up to a theory of language and behavior: an ability to adorn with words the day-to-day ceremonies of living may indicate a life of profound wisdom." Meese (1987: 63) explains that, according to this theory, "language produces power and knowledge . . . it is the ability to interpret and transform experience." Plant (42) agrees: "the medium through which African Americans re-created and transformed themselves and their world was the spoken word." For Wall (1997a: 377), speech can be transforming because it can influence a speaker's

"self-definition," which Hemenway (277) describes as the "soulful essence" of speech.

Nonetheless, Hurston is not naive about our capacity for using speech to enhance a sense of self. She ridicules this capacity in *Their Eyes* after Amos Hicks boasts to Lee Coker that women are irresistibly attracted to him. "Hicks, Ah'd git mad and say you wuz lyin' if Ah didn't know yuh so good. You just talkin' to consolate yo'self by word of mouth. You got uh willin' mind, but youse too light behind" (38). Again, in the speech by Janie which concludes *Their Eyes*, Hurston generalizes that speech can be frivolous unless it involves appropriate acts and experience. "'Course, talkin' don't amount tuh uh hill uh beans when yuh can't do nothin' else" (1937/1998: 192). Indeed, Hurston later explains one cost of frivolity with an example from her own life. "For theatrical effect, I had uttered sacred words and oaths to others before him ["P.M.P . . . the real love affair of my life"]. How I hated myself for the sacrilege now! It would have seemed so wonderful never to have uttered them before"[6] (1942/1995: 210).

The most valuable type of affective energy for Hurston, then, involves more than regarding one's speech as embodying a satisfying sense of self. Rather, this type also involves a certain degree of enduring significance, which Washington (1998) describes as necessary for inner growth. "When Janie says at the end of her story that 'talkin' don't amount to much' [sic] if it's divorced from experience, she is testifying to the limitations of voice and critiquing the culture that celebrates orality to the exclusion of inner growth" (xv). A relevant test of whether a speaker's prayerfully delivered speech involves inner growth, of course, is whether her subsequent behavior can be reasonably well predicted. Notwithstanding its involving surrealistically juxtaposed images, that is, speech does not seem significant unless a speaker's subsequent behavior develops as might seem reasonably indicated by such speech. Thus, Turner's description of role-enactments, considered in chapter 1, as enhancing the predictability of a speaker's behavior provides a significant test of whether her speech involves inner growth. This type of test seems especially relevant for people with unusual sensitivity to the images, or roles, by which another person can be interpreted in a given situation.

5. Performism

Both Senghor and Hurston recognize their views might be true of those who are not Black. For Senghor, the point is implicit in his explication of affective energy. "Let us return, as always, to the emotive power of the African, white or black: to the intensity of his affective energy, accumulated as in a battery" (1971: 43). For Hurston, the point is explicit in a letter to Burroughs Mitchell (her Scribner's editor for *Seraph on the Suwanee* [1948/1991]) on 2 October 1947, as quoted by Carby (1991: ix).

> They [Southerners] go for the simile and especially the metaphor. As in the bloom of Elizabethan literature, they love speech for the sake of speech. This is common to white and black. . . . [N]o Yankee can stand up to him [a white Southern politician] so far as compelling language goes. . . . They did *not* get it from the Negroes. The Africans coming to America got it from them.

Furthermore, Hurston's view is often criticized as not typically true of Blacks outside a rural, all-Black, Southern community. Likewise, Senghor's view is often criticized as not typically true of those who are not Francophone, intellectual Africans. It would thus be unnecessarily contentious to regard any of the features of speech considered by Senghor or by Hurston as uniquely true of Africans, African Americans, Negroes, or Blacks.

On the other hand, both Senghor and Hurston emphasize certain features of speech as used by those among whom everyone is an actor. This is an apparently noncontentious feature that Hill suggests be developed with the dramaturgical concept of role-enactment: performance. Let us therefore focus on social performance in developing our own view of language as involving some of the most important features of speech discussed by Senghor or by Hurston.

Of course, a person's performances in everyday life typically seem different, less posed and nuanced, than those in staged, theatrical productions. It might therefore seem misleading to regard any view gleaned from Senghor's or from Hurston's discussions of speech as true of those designated simply as performers. Instead, let us label them *performists* and identify them in terms of how they employ speech.

Performism Summarized

Performist speech contains some but not all of the features emphasized by Senghor and by Hurston. Most importantly, performist speech is like that which they consider in emphasizing a speaker's affective energy, her ability to speak so as to enhance a sense of self. This is the sense of "soul" Senghor and Hurston attribute to a person, as this concept is explicated for them by commentators such as Hemenway and Plant. It is described thus regarding speech in professional acting: "Within the realms of the imagination we can create things. . . . Through the dramatic act, the actual embodiment of imaginative constructs through enacting them in front of an audience, an infinity of possibilities can be brought to life"[7] (Grainger and Duggan, 1997: 126).

By taking advantage of this fact, Senghor and Hurston observe a speaker can amplify, and Hurston observes she can also diminish, various senses of herself.

The remainder of this monograph is concerned with developing those observations. In doing so, it adopts a suggestion by Hill (1996), North (1994), and Plant (1995) that this sort of thing incorporate some of the discussion about Austin's concept of illocutionary speech-acts.[8] Specifically, we will see that speakers can enhance their senses of self by identifying themselves with the illocutionary attitudes embodied in their speech-acts. This can and must be done "conventionalistically" as well as "intentionalistically." We will also incorporate the internalistic/externalistic distinction developed by the dramaturgical approach to social psychology, as considered in chapter 1 above. On the one hand, a person can internalistically perform speech-acts so as to enhance a sense of self that is satisfying. On the other hand, she can externalistically perform speech-acts so as to fulfill what seem to be the conditions other people consider in understanding certain roles or momentary images.

In short, a performist can attend to her senses of self by regarding them as the illocutionary attitudes embodied in her speech-acts. She can do this either conventionalistically or intentionalistically. In each case, she can do so either internalistically or externalistically.

Performism Is Different from Negritude and from Negro Expression
We agree with Senghor and with Hurston that the effectiveness of a person's speech-acts often depends on her affective attitude, her sensitivity to performance-inviting images associated with objects and with other people in various situations. Indeed, we have observed that the Method approach to professional acting recommends that speakers often employ their affective attitudes offstage as well as on-. But we also observe that Mamet, among other prominent acting theorists, rejects such employment in either venue. We conclude that some but not all people communicate well when speaking with an affective attitude. Performism as we understand it therefore allows but does not require that a speaker's affective energy be excited by her affective attitude.

Similarly, performism allows but does not require that a speaker's affective energy be excited by her understanding of spiritual entities such as departed ancestors. Senghor's view of this matter, animism, does provide an ontological grounding for Hurston's view of at least one form of speech, shouting in a

Black church. Namely, one then speaks dramatically from being impacted by external life-forces (or also, for Senghor, to appropriately excite her own and other life-forces, especially those of departed ancestors). But Hurston ignores any such grounding with respect to nonshouting types of speech, and so shall we with respect to all types.

Both Senghor and Hurston emphasize speakers for whom, relatively often, immediate experience takes precedence over analysis, and the personal over the theoretical. The type of performism of concern to us has no such emphasis. It is concerned with any speaker who regards the illocutionary attitudes with which she delivers speech as her senses of self.

Both Senghor and Hurston emphasize speech involving tropes that are relatively incomplete or strangely juxtaposed. They think such angularity tends to engage the active participation of listeners relatively much. Apparently, listeners then supply speech, which gives interpretation and direction to that in which a speaker has just embodied a given sense of herself.

The type of speech of concern to us includes but is not restricted to speech which involves tropes. Likewise, it includes but is not restricted to speech which involves images that seem incomplete or strangely juxtaposed. Though delivered in dialect, after all, Janie Crawford's speech is typically as "symmetric" as that of a Jane Austen character. We are concerned simply with speech that, when performed consciously, enhances a speaker's sense of self. What we will add to Senghor's and to Hurston's discussions of this is that a speaker can enhance her senses of self by attending to the illocutionary attitudes embodied in her utterances. She can do so conventionalistically as well as intentionalistically, internalistically as well as externalistically.

Notes

1. Indeed, Hemenway (121) emphasizes that Hurston's personal experiments with the American form of animism, hoodoo, distinguish her from most of the other Harlem intellectuals.

> In Hurston's case it [her novitiate in hoodoo] was earned by lying nude for sixty-nine hours, face downward on a couch at [Luther] Thompson's house, without food or water, with her navel touching a snake skin beneath her. . . . "My soul would be standing naked before the spirit to see if he would have me." . . . It is a suspended moment of high seriousness, of another order of existence from a night on the town with the Niggerati [a term which Hemenway observes is used especially by Hurston, Langston Hughes, and Wallace Thurman (her coeditors on a short-lived quarterly magazine, *Fire!*) for designating both themselves and the more established Black intellectuals]. One cannot imagine Alain Locke in the same position. It is the act of a dedicated anthropologist willing to place herself in both physical and psychic peril. One does not participate in such rites for pure

adventure. The act is not casual, and a person enters into it with fearful knowledge of its dangers and an anxious sense of its possibilities. It is the kind of act that separates Zora Neale Hurston from the Harlem literati and adds a different dimension to the sources of her imagination.

2. Marlon Brando, perhaps the most prominent Method actor, maintains that daily life inevitably involves our acting, using one set of techniques or another.

> The oldest profession in the world is not whoring, it's acting. This is not meant to be a pejorative comparison in any way. It is a simple fact that all of us use the techniques of acting to achieve whatever ends we seek. . . . Acting serves as the quintessential social lubricant and a device for protecting our interests and gaining advantage in every aspect of life. (1988: 1–2)

Though not a Method actor himself, Laurence Olivier (1982) agrees, at least concerning himself.

> Nowadays people often ask my wife, Joan [Plowright], "How do you know when Larry is acting and when he's not?" and my wife will always reply, "Larry? Oh, he's acting all the time." In my heart of hearts I only know that I am far from sure when I am acting and when I am not. (1982: 20)

3. Batson (2007: 106) agrees, "The place, like the person and the object, has to seduce you into experiencing genuine sensation."

4. One of my deans at the University of Calabar addressed the value of speech in more prosaic terms after a particularly long and rambling faculty meeting. In response to a later query, the dean explained he had allowed the faculty's penchant for oratory unusually free rein because he knew an important committee report would be an hour or two late. Anticipating the faculty's objecting to this irresponsibility, he expanded its access to the entertainment typically resulting from public oratory.

5. Sartre considered this when choosing "Orphee Noir," "Black Orpheus," to name his preface to Senghor's (1948) anthology of negritude poetry. "I shall name this poetry 'orphic' because this untiring descent of the Negro into himself causes me to think of Orpheus going to reclaim Eurydice from Pluto" (1948/1963: 21). The relevant element of the Orphic myth concerns the death of his wife, Eurydice, and Orpheus's subsequently following her to the underworld. By virtue of his musical skill, part of oral traditions, Orpheus there secured Eurydice's release. The one condition imposed by Pluto was that Orpheus not look at Eurydice while escorting her back to the upper world. When he eventually violated this condition, Eurydice disappeared from Orpheus forever. Sartre thinks a performist's speech enhances his search for self most fully only if he cannot fully anticipate its development. This occurs, for example, when one's speech is unusually influenced by that of other people, or is unusually free of rigid logical categories.

6. Boyd (2003: 271) identifies P.M.P. as Percival McGuire Punter, a graduate student twenty-one years Hurston's junior whom she initially met as a bit player in

one of her 1932 musical productions. Hurston wrote about two heroic lovers, Janie Crawford and Tea Cake Woods, while romantically involved with Punter: "I tried to embalm all the tenderness of my passion for him in *Their Eyes Were Watching God*" (1942/1996: 211). Howard (1987) therefore thinks Hurston views Janie as an autobiographical character. "It [*Their Eyes*] is a tribute to self-assertion and Black womanhood, the story of a young Black woman in search of self and genuine happiness, of people rather than things, the story of a woman with her eyes on the horizon . . . like Hurston herself" (140).

7. Messinger, et al. (1962/1990a) observes that focusing on oneself in terms of such constructs is not without dangers when done offstage. For example, it can evoke a sense of instability and anxiety. A person's

> character comes to appear to him as a "constructed object," as a "function" of manipulated activities and contrived scenes, of the assessments of an audience and the standards they invoke, and of the nature and availability of props. The connection between self and character becomes a questionable, undependable matter. (36)

Bob Dylan observes a related danger:

> I was singing words I didn't really want to sing. I don't mean words like "God" and "mother" and "President" and "suicide" and "meat cleaver." I mean simple little words like "if" and "hope" and "you." . . . It's very tiring having other people tell you how much they dig you if you yourself don't dig you. (1966: 42)

8. Austin analyzes any meaningful utterance as having at least three forces corresponding to three attitudes taken by speakers: locutionary, illocutionary, and perlocutionary. For the sake of argument, we rely on the following summary by Urmson (1998).

> The locutionary force is roughly the sense and reference of the utterance, the illocutionary force is what one is doing in making an utterance with a given locutionary force, and the perlocutionary force is the effect that is intended to be achieved by an utterance with a given illocutionary force. Thus the locutionary force of "The bull is charging" is simply the predication of something to an animal; the illocutionary force may be that of a warning, a comment on the scenery or an exclamation; and if the illocutionary force is that of warning, the perlocutionary effect intended may well be to make somebody run for it. (573)

CHAPTER THREE

Performatives and Reflexivity in Light of Hurston's Ethnography and Fiction

1. Conventionalism and Intentionalism

We are concerned with performism as a view of speech used to influence self-awareness. Within performism this can be done by a speaker's attending to the illocutionary attitudes embodied in her various speech-acts.

As introduced by Austin (1962) and by Searle (1969, 1989), the concept of illocutionary attitudes was interpreted conventionalistically, as will be explicated shortly. Eventually, the conventionalistic interpretation was superceded in popularity by an intentionalistic interpretation introduced by Grice (1957) and by Strawson (1964). This involved substantial debate between Searle and the team of Bach and Harnish (1979, 1992). We will examine some of that debate in this chapter. Using speech from Hurston's ethnographic folklore and fiction, this will show that some speech requires a conventionalistic interpretation while other speech requires an intentionalistic interpretation. Two prominent criticisms of conventionalism will be addressed in chapter 4.

Searle's Conventionalism
Searle thinks that, because of a convention, an explicit performative utterance helps to create "an act" or "an event" or "a fact" sufficient for making true the "propositional content" of that utterance. What is additionally required is that listeners have "uptake" in two senses. First, listeners must understand that, in virtue of this convention, someone's manifesting an intention to satisfy it, when recognized, "constitutes" a certain act so as

to "guarantee" its having been performed.[1] Second, listeners must actually recognize for what it is a verbal manifestation of a speaker's intention to satisfy this convention. Listeners do so most easily by recognizing that certain words, "warn" and "order" for example, "encode the intention to perform the act named in the sentence by the utterance of that very sentence" (1989: 552). When both conditions are met in appropriate circumstances, saying something is doing the relevant thing. For example, saying "I warn that x," when understood in appropriate circumstances, constitutes a warning, an illocutionary act. According to Searle, this act is sufficient for making true the propositional content of "I warn that x." That is,

> the truth of the statement [associated with a performative utterance] derives from the declarational [performative] character of the utterance and not conversely.[2] In the case of [all explicit—cf. note 9 of chapter 4] performative utterances, the assertion is derived from the declaration and not the declaration from the assertion. (1989: 553–54)

This position is generally known as conventionalism.

The Intentionalism of Bach and Harnish

Bach and Harnish agree that addressee-uptake of a speaker's intention to satisfy certain conventions with speech is sufficient to change the world relevantly. These are the "extralinguistic" kind not found among those governing speech itself. In virtue of an extralinguistic convention, for example, Bach and Harnish agree that an appropriately placed and understood pastor's uttering "I pronounce you man and wife" creates a marriage. But Bach and Harnish deny this is true of the more common kind of performative governed only by the usual conventions concerning locutionary acts, so-called linguistic performatives—someone's uttering "I order that x," is one of their examples. (Presumably, Bach and Harnish intend for us to consider this example outside contexts, military ones for example, which involve extralinguistic conventions about the use of "order." Even a restaurant order, however, involves extralinguistic conventions. "I warn that x" seems a clearer example of a linguistic performative.)

Instead, Bach and Harnish maintain a related combination of two things is required for the communicative success of a linguistic performative. This rather complex, subtle, and personal combination is required because Bach and Harnish think such performatives are basically acts of communication which, when successful, express a speaker's illocutionary attitude (warning or ordering, for example) in a certain way. First, a speaker must reflexively intend that, in virtue of recognizing her utterance as thus intended, addressees recognize it as expressing a certain illocutionary attitude.

Indeed, as Grice (1957) discovered, it is included in your intention that the audience take you to intend them to recognize it and that this be part of their basis for recognizing it. This "reflexive" intention constitutes the utterance as an act of communication. . . . [C]ommunicating is the act of *expressing an [illocutionary] attitude*. . . . We define expressing an [illocutionary] attitude as reflexively intending the addressee to take one's utterance as reason to think one has that attitude. (1992: 95)

Second, addressees must have uptake. They must indeed recognize this reflexive intention for what it is. Once addressees recognize this, the world is relevantly changed. But this change depends on addressee-recognition of the speaker's reflexive intention to express something advanced as true, a statement or assertion. The performative success of the utterance thus depends on its being first understood as a statement.

[A] performative sentence when used performatively is used literally, directly to make a statement and indirectly to perform the further speech-act of the type (an order, say) named by the performative verb ("order"). (1992: 98)

This position is generally known as intentionalism. Of course, some intentionalists interpret a speaker's communicative intention differently than do Bach and Harnish. Davis (2002), for example, denies that a speaker's communicative intention must concern addressees. So far as I know, however, all intentionalists regard the illocutionary/performative success of an utterance as depending on its statemental success. For intentionalists, that is, the performative success of Smith's uttering, say, "I warn that the bull is charging" depends on Jones's recognizing that Smith reflexively intends for Jones to regard this utterance as involving the true statement that Smith intends to warn about a bull. Only after Jones recognizes this is a new and performative act created, a warning.

In sum, conventionalists and intentionalists construe in opposite manners the relationship of dependence between the performative and the statemental successes of any linguistic performative utterance. We reconsider this point at the end of section 4 below.

Difficulties in Describing Intentionalism

Before leaving this discussion of intentionalism, we should note certain difficulties in explaining how speech-acts might be characterized as involving intentions that are reflexive.

Perhaps most basically, Siebel (2003: 357) observes that Bach's and Harnish's view of reflexive intentions "makes demands too great on the psychological abilities of [some of the] persons who perform such acts"—children, in particular.

Furthermore, not even Grice is convincing about how reflexive intentions should be specified. For example, he typically claims that speech cannot be uniquely characterized by intentions unless they are reflexive in the sense described by Bach and Harnish above. In particular, we cannot distinguish between "'deliberately and openly letting someone know' and 'telling'" (383) without regarding reflexive intentions in that sense as uniquely characterizing the latter. Strawson's (1964) sympathetic discussion of Grice's analysis observes, however, that not even intentions which are reflexive in Grice's sense suffice for this. Strawson's proof is that a person, S, might avoid speech while still employing Grice's type of reflexive intention to deliberately and openly let someone, A, know something. "S . . . arranges convincing-looking 'evidence' that p, in a place where A is bound to see it. He does this, *knowing that A is watching him at work*" (446).

Strawson then observes that even a more complex sense of reflexive intentions he develops to distinguish these two cases "is not *sufficient* to constitute the case." Instead of identifying what does suffice, Strawson says "I shall rest content for the moment with the fact that this addition at least is necessary" (447). In developing the conclusion of his argument, however, Strawson later maintains "It would equally be a mistake . . . to generalize the account of illocutionary force derived from Grice's analysis" (459). Strawson's reason is that this would involve a false "holding" with respect to his own way of specifying the intentionalism/conventionalism distinction considered in note 10 below. In other words, Strawson seems to think his modification to Grice's specification is neither necessary nor sufficient for "constituting" speech as "telling."

Nor is it easy to specify even whether speech is uniquely characterized by intentions of any type. Grice himself implies there is sometimes no intention-based difference on which to base a distinction between deliberately letting someone know something and telling it to her. "[T]hough in general a deliberate frown may have the same effect (as regards inducing belief in my displeasure) as a spontaneous frown, it can be expected to have the same effect only *provided* the audience takes it as intended to convey displeasure" (383). Grice thus acknowledges we can successfully communicate our displeasure not only by intentionally telling this to someone but also by intentionally letting her know it. (When the audience recognizes our displeasure from "spontaneous" frowns, Grice presumably thinks information is demonstrated, or some such, but not communicated.)

Also notable is that Grice's example concerns an intention which draws attention simply to a certain attitude, displeasure, rather than to the intention itself as well. In other words, Grice's example concerns an intention that is not reflexive as Bach and Harnish specify above. The same is true of Bach and Harnish. Sometimes, they focus on a communicative intention that draws attention simply to a certain attitude. "Ordinary performatives are acts of communication and succeed as such if one's audience infers one's communicative intention, the intention to be expressing a certain attitude" (1992: 94).

With these difficulties noted, let us continue to characterize Bach's and Harnish's preferred view concerning intentionalism as above. An utterance's communicative success for Bach and Harnish most often involves a speaker's reflexively intending that, in virtue of recognizing her utterance as thus intended, listeners recognize it as expressing a certain illocutionary attitude—warning or ordering, for example. This encapsulates their view that speech as communication involves a speaker's intending that this intention be recognized as evidence of her having some particular illocutionary attitude. "For S to express an [illocutionary] attitude is for S to R-intend [reflexively intend] the hearer to take S's utterance as reason to think S has that attitude" (1979: 15).

In sections 4 and 5 below, we observe that a viable sense of verbal intentionalism can rely not only on intentions which are reflexive but also on those which are not reflexive. In section 6, we extend to speech-acts Nagel's observation that nonverbal acts can be delivered with a second type of reflexive intention. For the moment, section 2 considers that communicative success need not involve our identifying a speaker's communicative intention at all. Even when communicative success does involve such identifying, section 3 considers speech-acts that should be interpreted conventionalistically rather than intentionalistically.

2. Hurston's Ethnography Shows That Communicative Success Does Not Require Our Identifying a Speaker's Communicative Intention

Bach and Harnish think "acts of communication" are successful only when a listener recognizes a speaker's communicative intention. "Their success requires that the intention with which they are performed be recognized by your audience" (1992: 95). This, however, fails to deal adequately with acts of communication that are intended insincerely.

The point is implicit in an observation by Plant (1995) about Hurston's (1935/1990) ethnography.

> By persistently defining John as "a nigger," Ole Massa attempts to render John a linguistic cipher. Each time Ole Massa yells to John, "'Member youse a nigger,'" John responds, "'Yassuh.'" John is well aware of the intended message as well as the perlocutionary effect desired by its sender. What the sender is not aware of is that John's response is coded and the code is decipherable only by John, who more realistically understands the situational context. Ole Massa needs to hear that John acquiesces to an existence of nothingness. He wants to believe that John continues to be submissive and that, consequently, he, Ole Massa, remains dominant. John's speech-act leaves in place, for Ole Massa, a false reality that allows John the figurative and literal distance to be spiritually as well as physically free.[3] (Plant: 46)

If we interpret John's uttering "Yassuh" in this example as an explicit linguistic performative illocutionarily expressing submission, then it counts immediately against the view of Bach and Harnish.[4] There is no good reason for John's truly submitting to Ole Massa's utterance construed as a demand or as an order. Thus, there is no good reason for John to express submission sincerely, especially since this will be his last interaction with Ole Massa. When John nonetheless utters "Yassuh" instrumentally to protect his physical freedom, then, there is no good reason for his reflexively intending that Ole Massa identify his communicative intention. Rather, the instrumental sense of John's communicative success results from Ole Massa's not identifying John's communicative intention. John successfully maintains his physical freedom by uttering "Yassuh." He successfully maintains his spiritual freedom by intentionally uttering it insincerely. "The Negro domestic plays the role of self-deprecating clown. . . . [T]his kind of duplicity is the only way by which human dignity can be maintained within the self-awareness of people in such situations" (Berger, 1990: 52).

In a different but related vein, Austin agrees that speakers can focus on expected perlocutionary effects while ignoring specific ways of identifying the illocutionary force of whatever utterance is used for achieving these results.

> Saying something . . . may be done with the design, intention, or purpose of producing them [perlocutionary effects]; and we may then say . . . that the speaker has performed an act in the nomenclature of which reference is made either (C.a), only obliquely, or even (C.b), **not at all**, to the performance of the locutionary or illocutionary act (101, emphasis added).

There is thus an alternative interpretation to that of Bach and Harnish with respect to their example in note 4. Under Austin's interpretation here, we could not utter "I ask you to leave" in normal circumstances without intending to cause an exit, for we could not but expect it to do so. We can be so accustomed to the usual perlocutionary result of a certain utterance as to take for granted this result will occur in appropriate circumstances. If that utterance so regarded does cause an exit, it has been communicatively successful in an obvious sense. This is an instrumental sense in which speakers focus on the typical perlocutionary force of an utterance while more or less ignoring specific ways in which its illocutionary force can be identified.

The Response of Bach and Harnish Is Not Adequate

Bach and Harnish object that the above discussion fails to recognize that a speaker's insincerity concerns his expressed attitudes, not his communicative intentions.

> If you think the speaker actually possesses the attitude he is expressing, in effect you are taking him to be sincere in what he is communicating. But there is no question about his being sincere in the communicative intention itself—what one can be insincere about is actually having the attitude one is expressing. The communicative intention must be identified before the question of the speaker's sincerity can even arise. . . . You can be unsuccessful in conveying your communicative intention . . . but not insincere about it. (1992: 96)

The key to this argument is its claiming a speaker's communicative intention must be identified before his communicative sincerity can even be questioned. The claim follows from the definition considered in section 1, that communicating is expressing an illocutionary attitude, which itself involves a speaker's reflexively intending for us to take his utterance as reason to think he has this attitude. Given such a definition, speakers simply cannot verbally express an illocutionary attitude without reflexively intending for us to recognize that intention. Even if this is true, however, the intention need not be sincere. Rather, it must simply exist. A speaker must really intend that we take his utterance as reason to think he has a certain attitude. For example, John must really intend that Ole Massa take his uttering "Yassuh" as reason to think John has a submissive attitude. This need not involve John's really having such an attitude, however. Furthermore, neither John's intention nor his expressed attitude is sincere if he does not actually have this attitude. Thus, Ole Massa's identifying John's communicative intention would prevent John's communicative success.

We might describe the situation in at least two ways.⁵ On the one hand, we might describe John as having one communicative intention that comprises two elements. The first is that Ole Massa will regard John as having a submissive attitude. The second is that this way of regarding things be false. Within such a one-intention description, John's regarding himself as not really submissive is necessary for his feeling spiritually free. On the other hand, Ole Massa's regarding him as really submissive is necessary for John's physical freedom. Ole Massa's identifying John's communicative intention therefore would entirely prevent his communicative success concerning physical as well as spiritual freedom. Given that, from his viewpoint, John's utterance *is* communicatively successful, this way of describing the situation is not viable.

On the other hand, we might describe John as having two communicative intentions concerning his utterance. That Ole Massa regards him as submissive is what might be called John's direct communicative intention. That this way of regarding things be false is what might be called John's ultimate communicative intention. Of course, John does not intend for Ole Massa to identify John's ultimate communicative intention. Without this as part of his entire communicative intention, however, John cannot regard himself as spiritually free while uttering "Yassuh."

Under this way of describing things, Ole Massa's identifying John's direct communicative intention would not prevent John's communicative success. Indeed, given the Bach and Harnish definition of "expressing an attitude," such identifying would be necessary for that success. However, Ole Massa's identifying John's ultimate communicative intention would prevent John's communicative success. In other words, John's communicative success requires Ole Massa's identifying John's direct communicative intention without identifying his ultimate communicative intention. Furthermore, the combination of John's direct and ultimate communicative intentions is itself insincere. Unless an intentionally expressed attitude is sincere, that is, the overall intention itself is not sincere.

Style as Affecting One's Speech-Influenced Sense of Self
Under either of these construals, John's communicative success requires that Ole Massa misidentify at least some of John's communicative intention. His communicative success involves Ole Massa's mistakenly thinking John intends to utter "Yassuh" to express submission sincerely. Furthermore, Plant's insight from chapter 1 explicates John's speech-act. Specifically, John intentionally uses speech in this manner to "transform" his sense of "self

and world." (Transforming one's sense of self with speech is, perhaps, done more easily with speech which is extended, as true of Carmichael's example in note 3 above, than with John's laconic type.) John intends to utter "Yas-suh" insincerely, perhaps in a manner he views as over-the-top, not only to maintain his physical freedom but also to "name" himself as a spiritually free person who defies a man he disrespects but fears.

Singer/songwriter John Prine confirms that, at least for some of those who use speech as social performance, a specific style of delivery can influence how one understands his own speech. Prine advances the point with respect to a style of delivery that was physically rather than psychologically induced. Specifically, throat-surgery and radiation forced him to sing thirty-year-old songs in new keys. "The songs got brand new to me. It was like they sent 'em to Earl Sheive and they painted 'em. . . . That was one of the upsides of going through that ordeal" (Prine, 2005).

Presumably, John the ex-slave deliberately chooses a musical key that expresses both his direct and his ultimate communicative intentions for speech with Ole Massa. He thereby gains both physical and spiritual freedom. While using speech perlocutionarily to maintain his physical freedom, that is, John nonetheless feels spiritually free as an actor who uses some musical key to embody the verbally expressed mock he intends toward an overweening antagonist.[6]

Interpreting John's speech in this manner also suggests a distinction relevant to Goffman's concept of role distance, as considered in chapter 1 above. For Goffman, we perform with role distance when we twist a role so that everyone recognizes our resisting the sense of self typically associated with that role. John, on the other hand, resists his role by twisting it so that only he (and, perhaps, certain like-minded colleagues) recognizes his resisting the sense of self typically associated with that role.

3. Even When a Speaker's Communicative Success Requires Our Identifying Her Communicative Intentions, They Can Be Interpreted Conventionalistically

We have observed that John might use linguistic performatives to deceive Ole Massa. Often, however, these are not used deceptively. Such cases need not involve an intentionalistic view of a speaker's communicative intentions, however. This is true of linguistic performatives that are used playfully but sincerely, for example. Playful performatives are focused on creating a shared truth (about play as emphasized) by creating a shared fact (that play

44 ~ Chapter Three

is emphasized). Consider, for example, the response to Charlie's caricature of courtship in *Their Eyes Were Watching God*.

> "Gal, Ah'm crazy 'bout you," Charlie goes on to the entertainment of everybody. "Ah'll do anything in the world except work for you and give you mah money."
> The girls and everybody else help laugh. They know it's not courtship. It's acting-out courtship and everybody is in the play (67).

The playfulness of Charlie's declarations here depends on their being recognized as intended to emphasize playfulness (and then being helped with laughter). The truth that his speech-acts perform playful declarations is a shared truth that depends on other people's recognizing such acts as having already performed such declarations. This recognition does not depend on listeners' first regarding these acts as implicitly advancing statements Charlie regards as true about his utterances as playful declarations. The cumbersomeness and weightedness of such an approach would prevent its seeming appropriately playful.

A similar but more complex point is exemplified by the first meeting between Janie Crawford and the man who will become her third husband.

> "De name mah mama gimme is Vergible Woods. Dey calls me Tea Cake for short."
> "Tea Cake! So you sweet as all dat?" She laughed and he gave her a little cut-eye look to get her meaning.
> "Ah may be guilty. You better try me and see."
> She did something halfway between a laugh and a frown and he set his hat on straight.
> "B'lieve Ah done cut uh hawg, so Ah guess Ah better ketch air." (Hurston, 1937/1998: 97)

Insofar as Janie intends that Tea Cake respond positively to her first utterance, she cannot easily present it intentionalistically. She cannot easily present it as advancing a true statement that, when understood as such, creates a new fact in the world, a query. Such a presentation would seem too cumbersome, too weighty. Janie could too easily be seen as brash beyond reason if inviting Tea Cake to recognize that she intends to state, implicitly, as true of herself that she questions his sweetness, the approach of intentionalists.

Of course, it is logically possible for Janie to present her utterance intentionalistically.[7] She could intend that her uttering "Tea Cake! So you sweet as all dat?" be understood primarily as advancing a true statement that, when understood as such, creates a new fact in the world. It is also possible that Tea Cake interpret Janie's communicative intention intentionalistically. In such cases, Janie's utterance would have successfully communicated her intention. But Tea Cake might well regard such an intention as off-putting rather than as engaging.[8] Presumably, Tea Cake's challenging response ("'Ah may be guilty. You better try me and see.'") results from his pondering Janie's meaning in just this way. After all, his previous speech is nothing but friendly and solicitous.

Instead, Janie's utterance is better understood as inviting Tea Cake's recognition to establish what she intends to view as true of herself, that she questions him, though playfully. Her utterance is better understood as making its statemental success dependent on its performative success. Presumably, Janie replies to Tea Cake's challenging response with her laugh/frown ambiguity because that challenge diminishes her sense of speech-embodied self as inviting his recognition to establish that she questions him in a playful manner.

4. A Speaker's Communicative Success Can Involve Our Identifying Her Communicative Intentions Intentionalistically

In more serious situations, on the other hand, speakers often seek more than a recognition of that which depends entirely on listener-uptake. Rather, there is a clear sense in which we sometimes intend for addressees to recognize our being independently embodied in, responsible for, certain illocutionary attitudes—invitings, offerings, complimentings, demandings, for example. In this sense, we intend for addressees to recognize that, even without such recognition, we would regard ourselves as embodied in the illocutionary attitudes associated with certain of our utterances. The point is illustrated when Janie finally confronts her abusive second husband Joe Starks as he lies dying of kidney illness: "Naw, you gointuh listen tuh me one time befo' you die" (Hurston, 1937/1990: 86).

Here, Janie's utterance seems intended primarily to reveal that which she regards as already true of herself—namely, regardless of whether John agrees or even understands, it is true that she demands his attention. Here, the cumbersome weightedness of an intentionalistically interpreted communicative intention is natural. More than does a conventionalistically interpreted intention, an intentionalistic interpretation forces a listener's attention onto the speaker's illocutionary attitude regarded as relatively independent. The demand, a new fact in the world, exists only after Joe recognizes Janie thinks it already true that she intends to demand. To understand Janie's utterance, Joe must recognize Janie regards the illocutionary statement associated with it as true independently of Joe's own understanding.

Reflexivity Is Not Necessary for the Performative Success of an Utterance to Depend on Its Statemental Success

Bach and Harnish emphasize that someone in Janie's position does this by reflexively intending, in virtue of Joe's recognizing this intention, that he also recognize her demand. Such an interpretation is reasonable. The intention it involves draws attention not only to Janie's demanding attitude but also to this intention itself. She thus seems doubly embodied in her utterance, doubly intent on its being recognized as embodying her sense of self. It is thus unlikely that such an utterance be delivered frivolously.

On the other hand, an authentic appearance of speech-embodiment seems achievable by Janie's intending simply that Joe recognize her demanding attitude. So long as Janie seems to intend this, she would seem responsible for that speech as an implicit demand. Whether or not she would seem similarly responsible with a frown or by arranging nonverbal evidence is irrelevant to her seeming responsible for a demand presented with speech intended simply to expose her demanding attitude. As observed at the end of section 1, Grice as well as Bach and Harnish sometimes seem to agree. Several cases considered by each concern an intention that draws attention to an illocutionary attitude without also drawing attention to itself.

Within either of these types of intentionalism, Janie primarily advances a verbal expression as true of herself regardless of Joe's uptake. For convenience, we transform it into an explicit performative, "I demand you listen, Joe." As understood above, the performative success of this demand depends on its statemental success. The utterance is presented as true of Janie and therefore, when successfully communicated, as creating a new event in the world, a demand.[9]

What is significant is that Janie's appreciation for the illocutionary force of her speech can therefore be more independent than if its truth depended on Joe's uptake as creating the fact which grounds such truth. After all, something entirely independent of Janie might prevent such uptake. A sudden bee sting, for example, might prevent Joe's understanding anything Janie says at all. Without Joe's uptake, however, there would be no performative success. Hence, under conventionalism, there would be no statemental success, no truth, for Janie's demand. Under intentionalism, in contrast, Janie can at least regard her utterance as advancing a statement she regards as true even without Joe's uptake.

Speech-Acts as Personally but Not Communicatively Successful
Of course, much speech seems intended instrumentally rather than conventionalistically or intentionalistically. Speakers then seem to seek a perlocutionary result without attending to the illocutionary force of an utterance at all. They seem interested in this result without seeming especially embodied in whatever illocutionary attitude might otherwise be involved by such speech.

Even when we think a speaker does attend to the illocutionary force of some utterance, it can be hard to determine whether she does so conventionalistically or intentionalistically. Both conventionalists and intentionalists regard themselves as embodied in the illocutionary force of their speech, but the former do so less independently than do the latter. The former seek to create a shared fact on the basis of which the correlative statement becomes true; the latter seek to create a shared fact by advancing the correlative statement as already true. The sense of self embodied in a conventionalist's utterance is thus more dependent on a listener's uptake than is true of an intentionalist's utterance. Concerning many utterances, however, it is more difficult for listeners to determine which type a speaker intends than it is when Janie demands that Joe listen or when Charlie plays at courtship.

It is relatively easy, on the other hand, for a speaker to determine whether she is embodied in the illocutionary force of some utterance and, if so, whether conventionalistically or intentionalistically. Strawson (1964) confirms the point while developing his own interpretation of performatives.[10] Strawson observes that an isolated person who bequeaths a gift might feel satisfied even if he expects no one will ever be aware of this bequest. He might "take some satisfaction in the thought [that he had 'made such and such a bequest'], even if he had no expectations of the fact ever being known" (449). Strictly speaking, Strawson is wrong about this. The reason is that legal rules govern bequeathing so that it can be "made" only when communication is successful. Furthermore, only a fatuous person would take satisfaction in thinking he had uttered bequesting speech without the possibility of actually bequesting. But the gist of Strawson's thought is right. It is more reasonably expressed as an isolated person's taking satisfaction in thinking he had explicitly declared his wish to make the bequest: "I wish I could make such and such a bequest." A person might, in other words, evoke a relatively satisfied sense of self by deliberately choosing a valued speech-embodied illocutionary attitude with which to address a situation of isolation. No such speech can be construed as communicatively successful, for there can be no listener-uptake. Still, the speaker might regard such speech as intentionalistically presenting a statement which is literally true, that he wished to make a bequest. He might therefore be unusually aware of his speech-embodied attitude, and hence of himself as at least relatively satisfied.[11]

Summary of Intentionalistically Delivered Speech-Acts
In sum, intentionalists can feel more independently embodied in their performative speech-acts than can conventionalists. Consequently, an intentionalist can use performatives in managing her sense of self more independently than can a conventionalist. This, anyway, when intentionalism and conventionalism are distinguished in terms of the priority between an utterance's statemental and performative successes.

Of course, the case is different when the intentionalism/conventionalism distinction is regarded as identical with the linguistic/extralinguistic distinction, as recommended by Strawson. As Strawson suggests in note 10, after all, listeners are perlocutionarily compelled by understanding a speaker's illocutionary intentions in an appropriate extralinguistic context. Thus, if the two distinctions are regarded as identical, listeners would always be perlocutionarily compelled by understanding a speaker's conventionalistically construed utterance in an appropriate context. Under normal conditions, then, the responses of listeners could not negatively impact the sense of self embodied in the illocutionary force of such an utterance.

But we have rejected this way of viewing the intentionalism/conventionalism distinction. Instead, we have adopted another view recommended by Bach and Harnish and, sometimes, by Searle—namely, the intentionalism/conventionalism distinction depends on whether an utterance's performative success depends on its statemental success, or vice versa. When the distinction is regarded thus, utterances can be presented intentionalistically as well as conventionalistically in extralinguistic contexts, and conventionalistically as well as intentionalistically in linguistic ones.

Strawson's example above actually illustrates that an utterance governed by extralinguistic conventions can be more reasonably delivered intentionalistically than conventionalistically. Strawson thinks an isolated man might "take some satisfaction in the thought [that he had 'made such and such a bequest'], even if he had no expectation of the fact ever being known." Surely a bequest is governed by extralinguistic conventions. But an isolated man cannot reasonably present it conventionalistically. After all, he could expect neither performative nor statemental success in the absence of listener-uptake. If he delivers it intentionalistically, however, he can at least regard the utterance as advancing a statement as true of himself, that he is bequeathing.

Given the caveat above, of course, the isolated man should instead regard an alternative utterance as advancing as true of himself that he wishes he could bequeath. In either case, the utterance is advanced primarily to present as true that which, if understood by listeners, would ground a new fact in the world. Speakers know this regardless of whether listeners do. For that reason, intentionalistic speakers can feel embodied relatively independently in the illocutionary force of an utterance.

5. Uchendu's Ethnography Shows That a Speaker's Communicative Success Sometimes Requires Our Identifying Her Communicative Intentions Intentionalistically

We have observed that it is typically difficult for listeners to determine whether a speaker feels embodied in the illocutionary force of her speech and, if so, whether she does this conventionalistically or intentionalistically. In many cases, that has no significant consequences. Sometimes, however, a speaker's communicative success requires our thinking she regards the truth of a performative utterance as independent of ourselves. This obtains with respect to oaths, for example. For listeners, what is then most relevant is whether, independently of their own understanding of it, a speaker seems to regard her oath as true in the sense of involving an obligation. Whether listeners recognize that someone's utterance intentionally satisfies the usual conventions about oaths, thereby establishing that a conventionalistically construed oath exists, is sometimes not so relevant for listeners.

The point is illustrated in a description of the Igbo of Nigeria presented by the distinguished Igbo ethnographer, V. C. Uchendu (1956). This is not to suggest there is some essential linguistic feature common to all Igbos, or to all Africans as well. Rather, Uchendu's presentation is unusually short and clear about a point obviously true of many people in many cultures.

According to Uchendu, many Ibgos typically view the world as a "marketplace" to be manipulated for self-advantage.

> The Igbo world is a world in which . . . survival demands some form of cooperation among its members, although that cooperation may be minimal and even hostile in character. It is a world in which others can be manipulated for the sake of the individual's status advancement—the goal of Igbo life. (20)

As a result, according to Uchendu, Igbos conduct rituals of "transparent living" in which a suspect person must repeatedly swear his or her fidelity.

> A stranger may be required to swear repeatedly to his host. . . . And patron-client relationships as well as doctor-patient relationships may be strengthened by repeated swearing of fidelity. . . . This demonstrable evidence of good faith is the pattern of behavior one would expect from a people who put so much value on transparent living and who are realistic enough to believe that some people will not live up to the ideal behaviour unless they are constrained to do so. (17–18)

The assumption here is that any lack of truth in a speaker's oath will reveal itself in his manner of speech if he is forced to present such speech over and over while confronting an investigator. Of course, this assumption sometimes fails, as illustrated by the case of John with Ole Massa. Typically, however, it succeeds at least when investigators are alive to the gestural nuances with which a speaker's intentions are expressed and influenced by their own gestural nuances, as is true of people with affective attitudes for example.

With respect to people who are alert, it is sometimes important for a speaker to seem independently embodied in her oaths even if they are only implicitly performative. It is thus important for speakers, sometimes, to be recognized as speaking intentionalistically—as intending, reflexively or not, to display an independent attitude of fidelity. It is important for their uttering, say, "I swear that x" to be recognized as primarily advancing a statement they regard as true of their illocutionary attitude, independently of how listeners regard it. This does not guarantee they will actually honor the oath in the way an understood utterance can, within certain extralinguistic contexts, guarantee the existence of an oath. Often, however, the apparently intentionalistic intention of a speaker is regarded as making this more probable. That is the basis of rituals such as those involved in Igbo transparent living.

6. Nagel's View of Communicative Success Involves Another Sense of Reflexivity

The above discussion of reflexivity concerns certain individual communicative intentions—namely, those drawing attention to themselves. Nagel (1969) helpfully discusses a related sense of reflexivity that concerns certain communicative exchanges. These are those with items in a given speaker's contribution that draw attention to previous items in that contribution. Nagel advances a "general schema" that he thinks "typifies human interactions" of this kind. Such interactions involve "a complex system of superimposed mutual perceptions—not only perceptions of the . . . object, but perceptions of oneself" (10). Referring to the work of Grice (1957) in particular, Nagel maintains "such reflexive mutual recognition is to be found in the phenomenon of meaning. . . . Sex has a related structure" (12). After considering Nagel's insights regarding reflexive mutual recognition within sex, we will extend them back to speech.

By focusing on a sexual example, Nagel explains why interaction involving superimposed, reflexive mutual recognition is unusually significant for anyone participating in it. "[I]t gives him a sense of embodiment, not only through his own reactions, but also through the eyes and reactions of another" (11). Nagel considers Romeo and Juliet who, by virtue of an appropriately mirrored barroom, slowly become aware of each other as aware of each other. Step-by-step, they exchange face- and body-expressions that are recognized as displaying certain personal feelings. First, Juliet recognizes that she has aroused Romeo's sexual desire, as embodied in the expressions of his face and body. Second, as embodied in the appropriately modified expressions of her face and body, Romeo then recognizes that Juliet is sexually aroused by virtue of recognizing his own arousal. Third, as embodied in the appropriately modified expressions of his face and body, Juliet recognizes that his recognizing her arousal by his initial one enhances Romeo's initial arousal. What is salient for Nagel is that each person feels unusually "complete" when his or her sense of self, as "embodied" or "dissolved" in these personal expressions, seems confirmed by each such exchange.

In other words, there are at least two types of communicative embodiment that involve reflexivity. The first is that suggested by Bach and Harnish. We feel unusually embodied in our speech-acts when we attend to our illocutionary attitudes. The second is that suggested by Nagel. A person feels speech-embodied when the following two things occur. On the one hand, the sense of self embodied in her previous speech is confirmingly superimposed by the sense of her apparently displayed in an addressee's response. On the other hand, another apparently confirming superimposition results from the initiator's replying to the previous superimposition.[12]

This expands Senghor's (1965/1979: 32) contention that a speaker from an oral tradition often "is born-with and thereby knows the Other." Such "rebirth" results because the speaker identifies herself, at least partly, in terms of how she is addressed by those who witness her self-revealing acts of communication. Nagel's basic idea is that a sexual activity (such as shoe fetish) is "perverse" if it precludes access to felt completeness via this type of superimposed, reflexive mutual recognition.

Nagel thinks "on-going, self-confirming" systems of superimposed, reflexive mutual recognition are naturally extended from sight to touch. Performative speech-acts are another extension of such a complicated type of exchange, as is illustrated by Tea Cake's addressing Janie about a Sunday school picnic.

"Git yo' hat if you gointuh wear one. We got tuh go buy groceries." . . .
"Tea Cake, you sure you want me tuh go tuh dis picnic wid yuh?"[13]
"Me scramble 'round tuh git de money tuh take yuh—been workin' lak uh dawg for two whole weeks—and she come astin' me if Ah want her tuh go! Puttin' mahself tuh uh whole heap uh trouble tuh git dis car so you kin go over tuh Winter Park or Orlandah tuh buy de things you might need and dis woman set dere and ast me if Ah want her tuh go!"
"Don't git mad, Tea Cake, Ah just didn't want you doin' nothin' outa politeness. If dere's somebody else you'd ruther take, it's all right wid me."
"Naw, it ain't all right wid you. If it was you wouldn't be sayin' dat. Have de nerve tuh say whut you mean."
"Well, all right, Tea Cake, Ah wants tuh go wid you real bad, but,—oh, Tea Cake, don't make no false pretense wid me!"
"Janie, Ah hope God may kill me, if Ah'm lyin'. Nobody else on earth kin hold uh candle tuh you, baby. You got de keys to de kingdom." (Hurston, 1937/1998, 108–109)

Here, Tea Cake seems unusually intent on successfully and unfeignedly expressing each of his communicative attitudes to Janie: an invitation; a declaration of indignation; a demand of more nerve; a declaration of appreciation. As a result, Tea Cake seems unusually embodied in what he says. Likewise, Janie seems unusually embodied at least in her last utterance.[14] Thus, both Tea Cake and Janie seem significantly vulnerable to the superimposition between his or her own sense of self and the way in which that is addressed by the other.[15] This is corroborated by the adjustments each makes in response to his or her understanding of such superimposition at a given moment. Because Janie's second utterance (gently) challenges the sense (embodied in his second utterance) of Tea Cake as truly wanting her company, for example, his third utterance demands more nerve from her. In other words, Tea Cake reacts with a reflexive demand after recognizing the superimposition between his previous sense of self and Janie's apparent sense of him. Because Janie's next utterance acknowledges the appropriateness of this demand, Tea Cake's final utterance declares his appreciating their profound type of communicative exchange.

Because Janie continues to share with Tea Cake many exchanges involving superimposed, reflexive mutual recognition, she satisfies "that oldest human longing—self-revelation" (Hurston, 1937/1998: 7). (The same is true of Tea Cake, though most critics focus on Janie.) She becomes aware of herself as embodied in those of her acts of communication that are successfully intended to induce recognition of the various self-revealing illocutionary attitudes she issues toward Tea Cake, whether reflexively or not. Then, Janie becomes more aware of herself by virtue of recognizing that Tea Cake comprehends (and perlocutionarily values) the illocutionary attitudes she self-consciously exposes to him. Finally, Janie becomes even more aware of herself by successfully displaying her reflexive reaction to the sense of herself apparently involved in Tea Cake's comprehension as superimposed onto whatever sense of self was embodied in her previous act of communication.

Intentionalistic Success as Associated with Perlocutionary Success

Two significant features characterize the case above. First, at least some of the perlocutionary success of Janie's and Tea Cake's speech-acts depends on their illocutionary success. The perlocutionary success of Tea Cake's (implicitly) inviting Janie to the picnic, for example, depends on her recognizing his speech as illocutionarily expressing an invitation which actually embodies a sense of himself. This example thus differs from that discussed in note 4. It differs from someone's uttering "I ask you to leave" for instrumentally gaining someone else's exit regardless of whether that utterance is identified as an illocutionary request.

What is perhaps more interesting is a second feature of this case. Communicative success within it would be significantly diminished if the case involved illocutionary but not perlocutionary success. If Janie recognizes but is not appropriately aroused by Tea Cake's demanding more nerve from her, for example, then Tea Cake does not achieve the sort of communicative success he seeks. There is then no encouragement to his sense of embodiment in this kind of self-consciously expressed gesture. A subsequent deepening of this sense is thus less likely. In Hurston's terms, Tea Cake's soul would be less than fully developed, because less than fully revealed.

The view of Bach and Harnish thus seems slightly misdirected. As observed in note 10, their view focuses on communicative success as involving illocutionary but not perlocutionary success. We have seen, however, there are many linguistic cases in which communicative success, as both speaker- and addressee-identified, does not require an addressee's recognizing a speaker's illocutionary attitudes at all. On the other hand, such recognition does not typically conclude the unusually serious cases in which communicative success does involve an addressee's recognition of a speaker's illocutionary attitudes.

Rather, these unusually serious cases typically involve the addressee's responses as well; ideally, as expressing appreciation. They also involve, that is, perlocutionary success.

In short, Bach and Harnish are right that, at least sometimes, "communicating is the act of [reflexively] *expressing an* [illocutionary] *attitude.*" What they ignore is that communicating in their reflexive sense is most appropriate in unusually weighty situations involving an exchange of attitude-expressions.

7. Conventionalism, Intentionalism, Internalism, and Externalism

In sum, Hurston's ethnographic fiction about Charlie's playful courtship shows that a speaker's communicative success when sincere need not involve his communicative intentions as intentionalistically construed. The same is true of Janie's asking about Tea Cake's name. These items show that communicative success for sincere speakers need not involve their being recognized as intending to constitute a new event in the world, a query for example, in virtue of presenting the relevant utterance primarily as a statement which is true of their illocutionary attitudes.

On the other hand, Uchendu's ethnography about Igbo transparent living shows that a speaker's communicative success sometimes must apparently involve communicative intentions as intentionalistically construed. Likewise Hurston's fiction about Tea Cake's demanding that Janie have enough nerve to say what she means, and about Janie's demanding that Joe listen to her, appear to involve communicative intentions as intentionalistically construed. Indeed, Hurston's fiction suggests that a speaker can intend this without intending it reflexively. Tea Cake's uttering "Have de nerve tuh say whut you mean," for example, seems to present its performative success as dependent on its statemental success even when we interpret Tea Cake as intending simply that Janie recognize his demanding attitude.

Under either interpretation, Tea Cake seems somewhat independently aware of the embodied attitude in virtue of which the statement associated with his utterance is true. He seems intent on showing he independently regards the utterance as presenting a true statement concerning his demanding attitude. Tea Cake's speech presents to Janie a relatively independent sense of himself he apparently intends for her to recognize. Because her speech superimposes a confirming sense of him, his next utterance reflexively develops such embodiment. When exchanges of speech seem to involve such superimposed, reflexive mutual recognition, they tend to seem unusually complete.

Thus, Bach and Harnish are right in affirming, and Searle is wrong in denying, that speakers sometimes achieve communicative success when they (reflexively) intend for the world to be changed by an explicit linguistic performative advanced as true. This occurs when addressees recognize that a speaker (reflexively) intends to be recognized as presenting a true statement about some illocutionary attitude. People typically intend, and expect, this when they are unusually serious with each other. By speaking thus in concert with one another, people cannot only reveal but also develop their senses of self.

On the other hand, people can also do this when speaking conventionalistically, when they intend to create new facts in virtue of which the correlative statements are made true. This occurs, for example, when people play at some role. Searle is thus right in affirming, and Bach and Harnish are wrong in denying, that an explicit linguistic performative can be communicatively successful when we recognize that a speaker intends for its statemental success to depend on its performative success.

As is often true of debates, then, each side of the one above is right in what it affirms but wrong in what it denies. Of course, even Searle (1989: 535) acknowledges intentionalism is "the most widely accepted current view" of illocutionary acts. Since we are focused on performism as an approach to speech that involves self-awareness as this is gleaned from Senghor and from Hurston, this fact cannot be addressed adequately. As considered in section 8 of chapter 4, however, we can observe that one of the most prominent intentionalistic criticisms will have been answered by previous discussion in that chapter.

Relationships between Two Distinctions
The intentionalism/conventionalism distinction is related to that developed in chapters 1 and 2 between two dramaturgical interpretations of role-enactment. Under "internalism," a performist enacts roles, or momentary images, by managing the extent to which she regards the sense of self embodied in certain acts of communication as satisfying. Under "externalism," a performist enacts roles, or momentary images, by managing the extent to which her acts of communication conform to the conditions with which other people seem to understand those things.

Intentionalists about speech-acts can pretty clearly be internalists about role-enactments. Both regard a speaker's goal as revealing something true of her. What intentionalists emphasize is that, when understood, a person's speech-acts also yield new events in the world, demands or warnings or requests, for example. What internalists emphasize is that a person's speech-acts can also embody satisfying senses of self.

Bach and Harnish emphasize that intentionalists about performatives can also be externalists about role-enactments. They compare a person's using reflexive intentions in expressing her attitudes to a "game of charades." "[Y]ou decide to express a certain attitude and try to select words whose utterance will enable your audience, under the circumstances, to identify the attitude you are expressing" (1992: 104). In other words, Bach and Harnish think we manage speech-acts so as to conform to the conditions other people seem to think involved by a certain role, or momentary image, in terms of which we seek identification.[16] Intentionalists about performatives can therefore be externalistic as well as internalistic about role-enactments.

Conventionalists about performatives can pretty clearly be externalistic about role-enactments. Both regard a speaker's goal as fulfilling certain conditions of relevance for listeners. What conventionalists emphasize is that, when understood, a person's speech-acts create facts in virtue of which related statements are true of her illocutionary attitudes. What externalists emphasize is that listeners can thereby regard the speaker as enacting a relevant role or momentary image.

Perhaps most interestingly, conventionalists about performatives can also be internalistic about role-enactments. Charlie's caricature of courtship in section 3, for example, seems conventionalistically focused on creating a shared truth (about play as emphasized) by creating a shared fact (that play is emphasized). Creating this fact does not seem to depend on listeners' regarding the act as implicitly involving a true statement from Charlie about his illocutionary attitude as playfully courting. Nonetheless, the sense of self embodied in this playful speech-act seems satisfying for Charlie. Conventionalists about performatives can therefore be internalistic as well as externalistic about role-enactments.

Notes

1. We distinguish here between associating "in virtue of" with illocutionary force, and associating "by virtue of" with perlocutionary force. With several caveats, for example, Austin (122–31) recommends this distinction between "in saying" and "by saying." Bach (1998b: 82) puts the matter thus: "Austin . . . distinguished the act *of* saying something, what one does *in* saying it and what one does *by* saying it, and dubs these the 'locutionary', the 'illocutionary' and the 'perlocutionary' act, respectively."

2. Searle explicitly distinguishes declarations from performatives.

All performative utterances are declarations. Not all declarations are performatives for the trivial reason that not all declarations contain a performative expression, e.g., "Let there be light!" does not. But every declaration that is not a performative could have been one: e.g., "I hereby decree that there be light!" (1989: 550)

As observed in note 2 of chapter 4, Searle's discussion of "Let there be light!", while thought-provoking, is somewhat dense and subject to the criticism addressed to it by Bach and Harnish. For the moment, we observe simply that Searle does not distinguish the declarational and performative characters of a single speech-act. "A declaration is a speech-act whose point is to create a new fact corresponding to the propositional content" (549). "A *performative utterance* . . . constitutes the performance of the act named by the performative expression in the sentence" (537).

3. According to Hurston (1934/1970a: 27), John (or Jack or High John de Conquer) is "the greatest culture hero of the South. . . . He can out-smart everyone." Hurston (1935/1990: 90) depicts this specific interaction as occurring after John has gained his freedom by saving Ole Massa's two children from drowning.

> The theory behind our tactics: "The white man is always trying to know into somebody else's business. All right, I'll set something outside the door of my mind for him to play with and handle. He can read my writing but he sho' can't read my mind. I'll put this play toy in his hand, and he will seize it and go away. Then I'll say my say and sing my song." (1935/1990: 3)

Hurston quotes from no source in particular. Rather, she uses the device of unreferenced quotation to project her understanding of Negro expression onto those she thinks speak it. Stokely Carmichael reports this confirming dialogue from one of his voter-registration summers in Mississippi.

> "J.T.," the boss asked earnestly, "answer me this: Have we evah abused or mistreated you?"
> "Weal, Cap'n, Ah *cain't* really *say* as you has. Nahsah. Nah, you knows, I sholy couldn' *say* nothin' like that, Missa Charlie."
> "Good, good. An' ain't Ah always treat you fair? Ain' Ah *always* been right with you?"
> "Cap'n," the brother said thoughtfully, as though searching his memory, "you know, *I got to say* you has. Yessuh, I sho gotta say that. I *could nevah* look in your face and say yo' hasn't been good t'me. Nahsuh, Ah sho would never do that, suh."
> "J.T."—the boss beamed, confirmed in his own benevolence—"you a good ol' boy."
> "Mighty kind of you, suh," J.T. agreed. (Carmichael/Thelwell, 2003: 286–87)

4. A problem in treating "Yassuh" as an explicit linguistic performative, of course, is that it might not be understood as appropriately self-referential. Perhaps this problem can be offset by the fact that submission is sufficiently indicated by 'yes' that the term is used for denoting toadies who submit to everything, so-called yes-men. It seems arguable, then, that submission is indicated by John's uttering "Yassuh" as

much as a request is indicated by a host's uttering "I ask you to leave," Bach's and Harnish's example. "You could not utter 'I ask you to leave,' at least not in normal circumstances, without intending it as a request, for you could not but expect it to be taken as such" (1992: 105).

If readers nonetheless resist treating John's uttering "Yassuh" as an explicit linguistic performative, the example can be easily modified to show the same weakness in Bach's and Harnish's view. For "Yassuh," we merely substitute "I promise (or announce or declare) I will, Massa."

5. I am indebted to Timothy Chambers for this distinction.

6. Another side of this issue is presented by Preece (1936: 364), who argues that

> the Negro culture . . . has been one of evasion whatever its intrinsic beauty. The educational and economic limitations of a dominantly white society have forced the Negro to express himself in ambiguous terms. . . . [W]hile this quality is highly admirable for protective purposes, it obviously impedes further cultural development.

7. As observed in note 6 of chapter 2, Howard (1987) thinks Janie is largely an autobiographical character for Hurston. Alice Walker (1979: 1), however, suggests that Hurston herself was brash, sometimes beyond reason: "Zora Neale Hurston was outrageous—it appears by nature." Here, then, Janie cannot easily be construed as Hurston's autobiographical character. More importantly, Janie's conventionalistic communicative intention can be contrasted with the sometimes brash communicative intentions of an interestingly relevant person.

8. Again, Walker (1979: 1) finds this sometimes true of Hurston. "We do not love her for her lack of modesty."

9. Bach and Harnish deny "that the statement [associated with a given explicit performative utterance] is constitutive of the action [associated with that utterance]; rather, the statement provides the audience with a rational basis for identifying the action" (1992: 104). According to Bach and Harnish, then, the correlative fact need not be created even when we understand a performative utterance as a statement. Their reason is that the search for "a plausible explanation" of why a speaker issues the utterance as a true statement might still fail. Thus, our interpretation of this form of intentionalism in the text is simply that a new fact is created by a performative utterance when that utterance is communicatively successful, which involves its performative success as depending on but not as entailed by its statemental success.

10. "The pioneers of speech-act theory, Austin and Searle, advocated an institutional or conventional approach. . . . But an alternative, 'intentionalist' view, originating from Grice (1957) and Strawson (1964) developed, and is now the dominant trend in speech-act theory" (Recanati, 1998: 621). It should be noted, however, that Strawson's form of intentionalism is somewhat different from that of Bach and Harnish.

For the latter, "perlocutionary acts are not relevant to the present discussion" (1992: 95) of illocutionary success as involving a speaker's reflexive intentions. In concluding his analysis, however, Strawson emphasizes that perlocutionary acts are relevant to this. He emphasizes the point to help ground his way of contrasting speech which is intentionalistic from that which is conventionalistic.

> In the case of an illocutionary act of a kind not essentially conventional, the act of communication is performed if *uptake* is secured. . . . But even though the act of communication is performed, the wholly overt [perlocutionary] intention which lies at the core of the intention complex may, *without any breach of rules or conventions*, be frustrated. The audience response (belief, action, or attitude) may simply not be forthcoming. It is different with the utterance which forms part of a wholly convention-governed procedure. (458)

As indicated in section 1 above, Strawson then uses this way of distinguishing intentionalism from conventionalism to argue that his previous account of intentionalism, as derived from Grice's analysis, leads to a false holding.

> It would equally be a mistake . . . to generalize the account of illocutionary force derived from Grice's analysis; for this would involve holding, falsely, that the complex overt intention manifested in any illocutionary act always includes the intention to secure a certain definite perlocutionary response or reaction in an audience over and above that which is necessarily secured if the illocutionary force of the utterance is understood. (459)

11. Siebel (2003) observes that, insofar as the Bach and Harnish concept of reflexive intentions is directed to an audience, their concept of a speaker's communicative intention cannot cope with soliloquy. Instead, Siebel recommends the concept of Davis (2002).

12. Grice (384) observes that we can reflexively intend for a listener to recognize our having an attitude which is "cutting" rather than cordial. Likewise, while he regards it as less than "ideal," Nagel (14) recognizes an exchange of communicative acts can superimpose sado-masochistic speech-acts on one another.

13. Hurston (1942/1996) indicates the importance of an explicit declaration of affection concerning her "real love affair" with Percy Punter.

> As I said, I loved, but I did not say so, because nobody asked me. I made up my mind to keep my feelings to myself since they did not seem to matter to anyone else but me. . . . Then he gave me the extreme pleasure of telling me right out loud about it. (206–207)

14. Under one view, Janie also seems embodied in her first two utterances. Under it, there are at least three reasons why she genuinely doubts the most obvious meaning of Tea Cake's invitation. First, Tea Cake has already boasted about his exploits concerning physical pleasure with women in general (104). Janie therefore has wondered if "he's livin' wid some woman or 'nother and takin' me for uh fool" (106). Second, Tea Cake has been absent unusually long since his last meeting with Janie, during which they had slept together for the first time. Third, Janie is a rich widow twelve years senior to a traveling laborer/musician/gambler. Under this view, Janie's first two utterances genuinely seek an explicit verbal declaration in place of Tea Cake's implicit declarations and nonverbal behavior. Under this view, these utterances embody Janie's asking something of import for her.

A defect in viewing Janie as embodied in at least the second of these utterances is that it involves a false claim about her, that she does not mind Tea Cake's taking another woman to the picnic. Furthermore, Tea Cake has previously declared the depth of his affection. "Ah didn't aim tuh let on tuh yuh 'bout it, leastways not right away, but . . . You got me in de go-long" (105). Finally, Tea Cake has uncharacteristically earned enough money to pay for the shopping expedition. For such reasons, Janie's two queries might seem instruments of somewhat coy banter not embodying a weighty sense of herself.

15. Bach (1973: 64) endorses this view of such superimpositions, but notes they can be even more complicated: "What he ['a reflexively conscious being capable of changing myself'] thinks of himself is subject to modification in light of what he thinks others think of him, and what he thinks others think of him is affected by what he thinks of himself."

16. Bach and Harnish therefore think intentionalists approach speech in much the way Brissett and Edgley (1990a) think "the dramaturgically aware individual" does. Brissett and Edgley (17) quote Miller (1984: 143) to emphasize that such an individual

> not only intends to perform the action necessary to his role but also intends to *appear* in a particular way while or through carrying out these actions. . . . To act in this dramaturgical or *expressive* sense . . . is to act on the basis of a second-order expressive intention—the intention to appear in a particular way, describable in terms of the actor's culture-laden self-representation.

In other words, Brissett and Edgley think "dramaturgical awareness allows impression-formation to become impression-management" (17). Bach and Harnish think an intentionalist manages audience-impressions by presenting the performative success of her utterances as depending on their statemental success. As considered in section 5, this type of management is often necessary for an oath to achieve the perlocutionary result intended by its speaker.

CHAPTER FOUR

Exchanges of Speech

1. Magic, Performatives, and Conventions

The previous chapter considers Strawson's case in which a person's verbal expressions might influence her senses of self without depending on addressee uptake. In the Introduction, we considered related cases involving condemned political prisoners. When examining how a person's utterances might influence her senses of self, however, we more typically focus on exchanges of speech, ones requiring uptake and response by addressees. This is interestingly true of the discussion advanced by Fingarette (1972/1998) concerning what he thinks is the Confucian view of magic.

Fingarette's discussion is generally relevant to our previous considerations insofar as he thinks the Confucian view "has a new lesson . . . [for] Western thought" (vii) just as we think the views of Senghor and of Hurston do. Fingarette's discussion is specifically relevant to that in the previous chapter in three ways. First, it incorporates a conventionalistic interpretation of performatives quite similar to Searle's.[1] Second, the new lesson that Fingarette identifies as resulting from conventionalistic interpretations also results from intentionalistic interpretations. Third, just as we did in chapter 3, Fingarette emphasizes that many individual speech-acts should be understood as parts of a communicative exchange. In addressing this discussion, we expand the view of speech-embodiment considered in that chapter. The present one concludes by addressing two of the reasons why many philosophers now regard conventionalism as misguided.

Fingarette's Sense of Confucian Magic

Searle (1989) considers a concept of supernatural magic under which witches, magicians, and God can change extralinguistic features of the world simply by verbally declaring them changed. "When God says, 'Let there be light!', that I take it is a declaration. . . . It makes it the case by fiat that light exists" (549). Searle thinks this is one of the few cases in which, independently of extralinguistic institutions, the communicative success of utterances might create extralinguistic facts about the world. Bach and Harnish (1992: 101–102) respond that the extralinguistic transformation in such a case would involve "efficient causation" without involving communicative success at all.[2]

Without considering this dispute further, we observe that its supernatural concept of magic is a common one.[3] Fingarette, on the other hand, denies it is the type of concept involved by the Confucian view of magic. Instead, Fingarette maintains the Confucian view involves a purely natural account which "parallels" an Austinian insight about performatives—that, in virtue of certain conventions, "correct use of language is *constitutive* of effective action" (1972/1998: 14). In virtue of certain conventions, that is, "saying so makes it so" (1967: 41).

Fingarette expands this insight to cover all the conventions, nonverbal as well as verbal, within a single social "ceremony" or "ritual" or "practice"— Fingarette uses the terms interchangeably. He applies the point to handshaking or to being a father, son, teacher, or student as well as to promising, complimenting, pleading, or excusing in particular. In his most detailed illustration, Fingarette explains that, to satisfy normal conventions, a respectful student will not only display a certain warm reserve when shaking hands with a teacher but also fetch books when politely requested. "[Y]ou will spontaneously be rather obvious in walking toward me rather than waiting for me to walk toward you. . . . You will not slap me on the back, though conceivably I might grasp you by the shoulder with my free hand" (1972/1998: 10).[4] When they are understood, nonverbal acts and inactions such as these literally constitute a person's being a respectful student, according to Fingarette. They do so just as someone's uttering "I warn that the bull is charging" constitutes a warning when it is understood. In virtue of certain conventions, certain acts performed and understood in certain contexts literally constitute a person's having a given "pattern" for Fingarette.

So long as we do this "with seriousness and sincerity," Fingarette thinks our conforming to the conventions concerning any pattern within a given social ceremony is effortless. "In well learned ceremony, each person does what he is supposed to do according to a pattern. My gestures are coordinated harmoniously with yours . . . all effortlessly" (1972/1998: 7). It is in this sense that Fingarette thinks some of our acts should be regarded as magical. "By 'magic' I mean the power of a specific person to accomplish his will directly and effortlessly through ritual" (3).[5] Thus, magical spirit "is no longer an external being influenced by ceremony; it is that that is expressed and comes most alive in the ceremony" (16). Magic is performed rather than externally introduced (by the life-forces of departed ancestors for example) when we seriously and sincerely conform to the conventions concerning our patterns, or roles, within a given ritual; and hence do so effortlessly.

Roles as Patterns of Behavior for Fingarette
In viewing one's roles as patterns of behavior for Fingarette, we adopt Turner's explicit treatment. "Role refers to a pattern which can be regarded as the consistent behavior of a single type of actor" (1962/1990: 99). While Fingarette uses 'pattern' much more often than 'role,' he also seems to adopt Turner's type of treatment. He does so concerning such roles as being a prince or a father, for example. "[B]eing a prince, a father, a son and so on" involves "truly human patterns" (1962/1990: 14). Insofar as we view our social roles as social forms, Fingarette also seems to accept Turner's type of treatment concerning the Confucian concept of li, which Fingarette explicates as "social forms." "Li refers to the . . . overt and distinguishable pattern of sequential behavior" (42). Finally, Fingarette's one explicit and relevant use of "role" seems to adopt Turner's type of treatment. "[N]o word alone, independent of ceremonial context, circumstances and roles can be a promise" (14).

Of course, the concept of a person's roles in social rituals would benefit from a great deal more discussion. For the sake of brevity but with relevance for Fingarette, let us treat our roles in social rituals simply as patterns of behavior. Let us also consider student-teacher and parent-child relationships as examples that involve social rituals.

2. Conventionalistically Interpreted Performatives as Relatively Effortless

Before addressing other concerns with Fingarette's discussion, we must observe it involves a relevant ambiguity. Fingarette repeatedly describes magical performances as being effortless. In the same discussion, however, he rightly recognizes that any magical performance involves "purely physical motion" (14); and thereby, surely, some amount of effort. The charitable interpretation would seem to be that Fingarette is most focused on a relative sense in which magical performances might be regarded as effortless.

Even under this relativistic assumption, Fingarette has no linked discussion explicating any specific sense of effortlessness. A viable sense might nonetheless be gleaned from his emphasizing in various places that a correct use of language can be constitutive of effective action. Fingarette (1967: 44) thinks this is true not only of explicit performatives but also of what Austin sometimes calls implicit performatives. When someone's uttering "I'm very unhappy about it" is understood in appropriate circumstances, for example, Fingarette thinks it typically constitutes an apology as much as does her uttering "I apologize." The reason is that both utterances "allude" to the same social practice, that of apologizing. As observed in note 1, that is, Fingarette thinks each utterance performs an apology in virtue of alluding to the same rule or convention of the form "Doing A in circumstances B counts also as doing C." Their difference is that "I'm very unhappy about it" alludes "tacitly" while "I apologize" alludes "explicitly."[6]

The most obvious sense in which an utterance is relatively effortless within Fingarette's discussion is the sense in which, as properly understood in terms of a relevant convention, that utterance constitutes a certain "further act" (1972/1998: 14). "The performative use of language constitutes . . . both the act of uttering words and the act of, e.g., apologizing" (1967: 45). The point is perhaps better expressed in Austin's nomenclature: When understood, an explicit performative utterance constitutes not only a locutionary act presenting sense and reference but also an illocutionary act of, e.g., apologizing.[7]

In virtue of a relevantly understood convention and intention, that is, an illocutionary act's existence is guaranteed by the existence of an appropriately delivered locutionary act. Indeed, Fingarette thinks this is true regardless of whether the utterance is explicitly or implicitly performative. Of course, the same act might be implicitly constituted in several different ways. The convention's benefit concerning explicit performatives specifically is its guaranteeing not only the illocutionary act's existence but also its identification, at least insofar as the convention and its terms are understood. In virtue of the convention, speakers can perform and listeners can recognize certain illocutionary acts relatively effortlessly. Relatedly, of course, Searle observes the illocutionary success of someone's uttering "I apologize," for example, changes the world so that the propositional content of this utterance becomes true. The utterance construed conventionalistically is thus relatively effortless in the sense that two "further results" depend on its locutionary success.

A Third Result That Depends on Locutionary Success

Just as saying so makes it so for implicit as well as for explicit performatives when they are understood, Fingarette thinks certain nonverbal acts can make things so when they are understood. For example, he thinks that, in virtue of our understanding the relevant social convention, a student's fetching books after a teacher's request constitutes the student's being respectful. Such respect can be otherwise constituted, of course. But doing this under a specific convention is relatively effortless. So long as observers understand the convention and its terms, someone's being recognized as intentionally satisfying it guarantees the respectful act's existence as specifically and properly identified.

Fingarette thinks this has a significant consequence for our participation in social rituals. The reason is that a social ritual is an interlocking sequence of patterned acts whose ongoing existence depends on there being a previous act which is well-identified concerning this ritual. "If all are 'self-disciplined,' . . . then all that is needed—quite literally is an initial ritual gesture. . . . [F]rom there onward everything 'happens'" (1972/1998: 8). Participating verbally or nonverbally in a ritual can be relatively effortless in the sense that we, as seriously and sincerely involved with certain conventions, know what to do in response to a well-identified and relevant act. This is a third further result that can depend on the locutionary success of a speech-act.

As observed in note 10 of chapter 3, Strawson advances a related point in distinguishing between "procedures" involving extralinguistic conventions and those involving only linguistic conventions. Specifically, he affirms of the former but denies of the latter that if "uptake is secured, then any frustration of the wholly overt intention of the utterance (the intention to further the procedure in a certain [perlocutionary] way) must be attributable to a breach of rule or convention" (1964: 458). In other words, Strawson agrees with Fingarette that our participation in a practice/procedure can be relatively effortless when it involves extralinguistic conventions. As critically discussed in section 7 below, Fingarette also thinks our participation in a practice/procedure can be relatively effortless even when it involves only linguistic conventions.

3. Intentionalistically Interpreted Performatives as Relatively Effortless

In chapter 3, we observed that some utterances invite a conventionalistic interpretation, but that others invite an intentionalistic interpretation. What is interesting is that our speaking intentionalistically is relatively effortless in roughly the way our speaking conventionalistically is. Specifically, three further results depend on locutionary success. The first is illocutionary success. Of course, Bach and Harnish think locutionary success never "entails" or "guarantees" illocutionary success when we speak intentionalistically. Rather, they compare speech to a game of charades in which one's speech serves as "evidence" from which audiences can infer "what you have in mind. . . . [T]he audience identifies the act being performed by way of understanding the statement being made and seeking a plausible explanation for the fact that the speaker made it" (1992: 96, 104). Such searches are "defeasible," not "deductive" (100).[8] Because such statements are "self-identifying," however, Bach and Harnish think such a search is relatively effortless with respect to utterances that are explicitly performative. In virtue of this, "the act named by the performative verb may be inferred from the statement" even though it is "not . . . constituted by the statement" (100). In addition to locutionary success, that is, communicative success for intentionalists also requires our recognizing the truth of a presupposed statement concerning some illocutionary attitude, something inferred from but not guaranteed by a speaker's locutionary success.

Recognizing the truth of a presupposed statement about a speaker's illocutionary attitude is the primary further result of an utterance's locutionary success when interpreted intentionalistically. Another, of course, is the one identified by Bach and Harnish in chapter 3, that the correlative fact is thereby created. Our speaking intentionalistically is therefore relatively effortless in the sense that two further results can depend on an utterance's locutionary success, though the logical priority between those two results for intentionalists is different from the logical priority between them for conventionalists.

For Bach and Harnish, another difference is that these results follow in a manner which is defeasible rather than deductive even for linguistic performatives which are explicit. As observed above, however, Bach and Harnish think our search for "a plausible explanation" concerning an explicit performative is relatively effortless because such an utterance is "self-identifying." In virtue of this, the illocutionary act named by the performative verb may be defeasibly inferred from the statement even though the statement does not constitute the act. When a speaker advances explicit performatives, even an intentionalistic audience can therefore identify them relatively effortlessly.

Again, then, participating in a social ritual can be relatively effortless in the sense that we know what to do in response to a well-identified and relevant act. This is a third further result that can depend on the locutionary success of a speech-act construed intentionalistically.

4. The Conventionalism/Intentionalism Distinction Concerning Implicit Performatives

Given the discussions by Fingarette and by Bach and Harnish, the difference between conventionalistic success and intentionalistic success is somewhat subtle concerning implicit performatives. On the one hand, Bach and Harnish regard illocutionary success as defeasible whenever people communicate intentionalistically. On the other hand, Fingarette agrees with this at least for conventionalistically intended performatives that are implicit. In particular, Fingarette thinks an implicit performative is communicatively successful in virtue of its alluding to some convention, though it does so only tacitly. Fingarette thus thinks listeners who identify a specific convention regarding some implicit performative must do so defeasibly. This is significant in that many observers regard most of ordinary speech as composed of implicit performatives. "Whenever we say anything meaningful we are doing something: we are asking, explaining, ordering, describing, narrating, implying, warning, insisting, boasting, begging, and so on" (Magee, 1999: 120). Concerning most of it, then, Fingarette agrees with Bach and Harnish that identifying the illocutionary forces of ordinary speech is defeasible.

We have nonetheless observed a significant difference even concerning implicit performatives. Conventionalists think an utterance's statemental success follows deductively from its performative success, even when the latter is defeasible.[9] The truth of an implicit performative's propositional content for conventionalists thus depends on the correlative fact created by that utterance as understood by listeners. Without such understanding, not even a speaker can regard the propositional content of her utterance as true. The truth of implicit performatives for conventionalists is thus inevitably a shared truth if it exists at all. In contrast, intentionalists think an utterance's performative success depends on its statemental success. As a result, an intentionalistic speaker can regard the propositional content of her performative utterances as true even when listeners do not understand those utterances.[10] An intentionalist can therefore feel relatively embodied in such speech-acts even when they do not successfully call attention to her illocutionary attitudes.

A sincere person who presents speech intentionalistically might therefore continue to develop its consequences more than he would if presenting the same speech conventionalistically. This explains why Tea Cake can persevere in addressing Janie as he does concerning the picnic despite his knowing, as observed in note 14 of chapter 3, she has reason to doubt his current intention. Tea Cake can persevere in such speech construed intentionalistically because he can then regard its propositional content as true somewhat independently of what Janie thinks. For Tea Cake, the sense of self embodied in speech seems relatively independent of what Janie thinks.

In contrast, suppose a conventionalistic construal of Tea Cake's uttering "[D]is woman set dere and ast me if Ah want her tuh go!" Under such a construal, the truth of this utterance's propositional content as an implicit declaration of indignation would depend on Janie's thus recognizing it. Such recognition is not obviously forthcoming, however. Rather, Janie responds by suggesting that Tea Cake's pose of indignation deliberately avoids a direct response to her previous query (about his being sure of his invitation): "Don't git mad, Tea Cake. . . . If dere's somebody else you'd ruther take, it's all right wid me." In other words, Janie suggests that Tea Cake's pose of indignation might simply disguise his more basic interest in other women. As intended by Tea Cake, then, communication would have failed; no declaration of indignation would have been created whereby the propositional content of that utterance becomes true. Whatever sense of self that utterance embodies would therefore be relatively extinguished just as was indicated in chapter 3 concerning the playful query Janie had previously issued about Tea Cake's name.

Relative to intentionalists, then, a sincere conventionalist is less able to develop the intended consequences of a speech-act when listeners seem not to endorse his or her way of identifying its illocutionary force. This is the most significant difference between construing one's implicit performatives conventionalistically and construing them intentionalistically. Both conventionalistic speakers and intentionalistic speakers intend for listeners to recognize some utterance as having a specific illocutionary force. Whereas conventionalists do this by construing the utterance's statemental success as resting on its performative success, intentionalists do so by construing the utterance's performative success as resting on its statemental success.

5. Performism as Related to Presentationalism and to Representationalism in Professional Acting

The conventionalism/intentionalism distinction, while not interchangeable with, is quite related to the distinction that results from what is perhaps the most prominent debate in contemporary thought about professional acting. The concept of affective energy helps to explicate one side of that debate which, in turn, helps to explicate the type of performism with which we are concerned.

This debate is often described as resulting from two factors. First, early twentieth-century European acting "had become very mannered" concerning such technical elements as "voice, diction, stance, movement" (Easty, 1981: 10, 178). Second, Konstantin Stanislavsky (1924/1948, 1936/1959, 1949/1969) taught a new approach to acting (popularized by such advocates as Stella Adler [1988], Uta Hagen [1973, 1991], Sanford Meisner and Dennis Longwell [1987], and Lee Strasberg [1987]), which emphasizes an actor's experiencing states of mind related to those expressed by the character he enacts. "Passionate debates ensued, which continue into the present, between those actors who espoused the new way of work—from the inside out—and those who defended traditional formalism—from the outside in" (Hagen, 1991: 47). Perhaps most helpfully, Hagen (1973) uses the contrast between "Representational" and "Presentational" to designate that between the traditional approach and the newer one.

> The Representational actor deliberately chooses to imitate or illustrate the character's behavior. The Presentational actor attempts to reveal human behavior through a use of himself. . . . [He] trusts that a form will result from identification with the character. (11)[11]

Laurence Olivier (1982, 1986) illustrates his use of representationalism with the following

> story of a young actor who went to London Zoo when he was about to play the part of the Fool in *Lear*. He was standing in front of the baboons, when he became aware of someone behind him. He turned and recognized an older actor. The older actor looked at him for a moment and then pointed at the enclosure. "When I played him," he said, "I was the one up in the corner with the red bottom." (1986: 23)

Most importantly, Olivier seeks those imitations that engage an audience. "A good actor is working in at least three levels at a time: lines, thought and awareness of the audience. . . . The actor must keep an audience engaged by constant changes of inflections" (19, 89).

For presentationalists, in contrast, "the first rule is that you . . . will ignore the audience and not worry about people watching you" (Adler, 1988: 31). Instead, presentationalists must literally experience something related to the states of mind expressed by the characters they enact; otherwise, "falseness" appears. Hagen (1973: 34) describes the process as involving "substitutions from our own experiences and remembrances." Presentationalists, that is, think the foundation of successful acting is "the desire to communicate one's own experience and sensations, to make one's self heard and seen" (Hagen, 1973: 13).[12] Presentationalists thus regard the acting in a dramatic performance somewhat as both intentionalists and conventionalists regard the acting in normal speech. In each case, a person intends to display some of her experience so that other people recognize it. For Bach and Harnish, this is the illocutionary attitude she has "in mind." The same is true of conventionalists, though they reverse the statement/performance priority of intentionalists in displaying these illocutionary attitudes. For Strasberg, what is displayed is a "proper sensory and emotional experience," whether from memory or from being "agitated" by items in some current situation.

Speaking Presentationally and Speaking with Affective Energy
Speaking presentationally is therefore similar to but also different from speaking with affective energy. Most significantly, they are similar in that each regards a person's speech-acts as importantly related to her senses of self. But they are different in how this is used.

One speaks presentationally by using speech-acts to express some inner sense of self when the primary purpose is to communicate more fully by making "one's self heard and seen." On the other hand, one speaks with affective energy when she uses a speech-act at least in part to enhance a felt sense of self for herself. As Senghor has observed, speech can be "the vibrating shock, the power which through the sense seizes at the roots of our being." Speech-acts involve affective energy within performism, in particular, when a speaker regards the illocutionary attitudes embodied by her speech-acts as her senses of self.

This is a reasonably clear way of being self-aware. It can feel significant when an illocutionary attitude is regarded more specifically than suggested by the items in Magee's list above: asking, explaining, ordering, describing, narrating, implying, warning, insisting, boasting, or ordering. Janie's (conventionalistically) asking "So you sweet as all dat?", for example, is not just a general form of asking. Rather, it is a specific form of asking, a playfully jesting one. Likewise, (intentionalistically) uttering "Ah wants tuh go wid you real bad" is not just a general form of declaring, but is instead a specifically wanting type of declaring. By focusing on the illocutionary attitude embodied by her speech-act, a speaker can either amplify or diminish an existing sense of self, or help to create a new one. Regardless, the sense of self is influenced by the tone and rhythm of her speech-acts, as would be appropriate when Janie shifts from offering Tea Cake an open relationship ("'Don't git mad, Tea Cake, Ah just didn't want you doin' nothin' outa politeness. If dere's somebody else you'd ruther take, it's all right wid me.'") to declaring her intensely wanting his attention focused on her ("'Well, all right, Tea Cake, Ah wants tuh go wid you real bad, but,—oh, Tea Cake, don't make no false pretense wid me!'").

Affective energy can also be used to interpret John's saying "Yassuh" to Ole Massa, though the case is more complex because the utterance is less sincere. On the one hand, John's utterance is representational and externalistic in that it imitates speech that typically accomplishes the perlocutionary goal he seeks, Ole Massa's regarding John as submissive. On the other hand, John's utterance involves affective energy in that, by virtue of tone and rhythm, it is intended to diminish any felt sense of submission otherwise embodied therein. Instead, by virtue of seeming over-the-top, for example, that tone and rhythm can be interpreted as amplifying a (disguised) illocutionary sense of self as mocking. Insofar as this sense of self is satisfying, the speech-act in which it is embodied is delivered internalistically.

Of course, John's speech-act cannot easily be performed presentationally to make his inner sense of self seen and heard. After all, this would diminish its representational effectiveness at imitating speech-acts that are typically successful at perlocutionarily convincing people such as Ole Massa of John's submissiveness. Professional actors, however, sometimes describe themselves as employing elements from representationalism in addition to elements from presentationalism. On the one hand, for example, Michael Caine (1997) is representational in sometimes imitating those items of other people's behavior that produce certain perlocutionary results unusually well. "When becoming a character, you have to steal. . . . You can even steal from other actors' characterizations . . . because what you're seeing them do, they stole" (88).[13] On the other hand, Caine is also presentational in depending on his emotional memory. "I could do it [dialogue, when the off-camera actor is engaged elsewhere] to the wall because I hang on to the emotional memory of how it was in the shot when he *was* there" (17).[14]

What performism emphasizes is that, in contrast with presentationalism as well as representationalism, speech-acts can be used primarily for a purpose other than effective communication. Rather, speech-acts can be used with affective energy primarily to enhance a speaker's senses of self. For a performist, this is accomplished by regarding one's senses of self as the illocutionary attitudes embodied in one's speech-acts.

6. Speech as Embodying a Speaker's Senses of Self

We have observed that speech-acts seem relatively effortless when a speaker focuses on her illocutionary attitudes and is thereby aware of herself as embodied in those acts. As Bach (1998b) notes, expressing some illocutionary attitude can be identical with expressing one's sense of self. Someone's uttering "I apologize," for example, can be not only "the act of . . . expressing a certain [illocutionary] attitude" but also "an act of expressing oneself" (84).[15] In recognizing the illocutionary attitude embodied in her utterance, that is, one can relatively effortlessly recognize herself, at least for the period of utterance, as embodied in apologizing. It is therefore curious that Fingarette sometimes disparages a speaker's consciousness of self when focused on a speech-act to express respect, for example, with relative effortlessness.

> This mutual respect is not the same as a conscious feeling of mutual respect. . . . [I]t is fully expressed in the correct "live" and spontaneous performance of the act. Just as an aerial acrobat must, at least for the purpose at hand, possess (but not think about his) complete trust in his partner if the trick is to come off, so we who shake hands, though the stakes are less, must have (but not think about) respect and trust. (1972/1998: 9)

Acrobats aside, we have seen that a speech-act by representationalists can, indeed, come off without their thinking of themselves as embodied in their speech. Before Stanislavsky, this was even the preferred approach to speech by professional actors in the West. But we have also seen that many professional actors now do think about their speech as embodying senses of self. Given the success of such Method actors as those mentioned in chapter 2, this obviously need not involve one's succumbing to the associated dangers, identified by Fingarette, of feeling "piously fatuous" or of seeming so to listeners. Presumably, performist speakers in ordinary life who employ affective energy need not succumb to these dangers, either. The characters in *Their Eyes Were Watching God* certainly do not seem to.

Given his concern with the relative effortlessness of certain speech-acts, it is doubly curious that Fingarette tends to ignore a performist approach to speech. It is curious that he tends to ignore our capacity for feeling self-embodied in speech. Speech as relatively effortless, after all, is something of which speakers are aware if it exists at all. Certainly, Fingarette seems aware both of himself and of other people in his role as respected teacher. Indeed, as observed in section 2, Fingarette emphasizes that everything happens relatively effortlessly if all of us in a given ritual are self-aware in the sense of being self-disciplined. "If all are 'self-disciplined,' . . . then all that is needed—quite literally is an initial ritual gesture . . . from there onward everything 'happens.'" Finally, Fingarette (viii) is concerned with "ideas . . . [which] favor the individualistic and subjectivistic view of man."

Perhaps Fingarette's fundamental position can be interpreted as suggesting only that our attention, if any, to a conscious feeling of mutual respect should be always dominated by our attention to the "'live' and spontaneous performance of the *act*" of respect. This interpretation is similar to one that seems appropriate for Mamet's discussion of the type of representationalism from which Stanislavsky departed.

Mamet criticizes representationalism for emphasizing poses and gestures that seem obviously narrated.

> In the theatre, as outside it, we resent those who smile too warmly, who act overly friendly, or overly sad, or overly happy, who, in effect, *narrate* their own supposed emotional state. Why do we resent it? Because we feel, rightly, that it is being done only to bring about or to extort something from us we would be reluctant to give in return for an uninflected presentation. (77)

Much of Mamet's constructive view of effective acting nonetheless focuses representationally on one's listeners as responsive, as "antagonists" with apparent states of mind.

> In "real life" the mother begging for her child's life, the criminal begging for a pardon, the atoning lover pleading for one last chance—these people give no attention *whatever* to their own state, and all attention to the state of that person from whom they require their object. This outward-directedness brings the actor in "real life" to a state of magnificent responsiveness and makes his progress thrilling to watch. On the stage, similarly, it is the progress of the outward-directed actor, who behaves with no regard to his personal state, but with *all* regard for the responses of his antagonists, which thrills the viewers. (12–13)

Because this passage emphasizes that a speaker "behaves with no regard to his personal state," it is difficult to interpret. As observed in chapter 2, after all, Mamet also thinks our speech should be "from the heart," something that involves a speaker's personal state of mind as sincere. As suggested there, Mamet apparently intends that our attention to speech-acts as heartfelt be always dominated by our attention to effectively communicating with the responses and apparent states of mind of addressees. Instead of being interpreted as suggesting we should never attend to our mental states while speaking, that is, Mamet might be interpreted as suggesting only that our attention, if any, to speech-acts as coming from the heart be always dominated by our attention to effective ways of communicating with the previous responses and apparent states of mind of other people. Likewise, Fingarette might here be interpreted as suggesting only that our attention to the "'live' and spontaneous performance of the *act*" of respect, for example, always dominate our attention, if any, to a conscious feeling of mutual respect.

7. Exchanges of Speech as Relatively Effortless

As observed in chapter 3, Nagel emphasizes that our senses of self can be embodied in our social actions. However, he thinks we feel more embodied when our social actions also involve superimposed, reflexive, mutual recognition with other people. This is what makes them seem "complete." We feel more fully embodied, for example, in certain exchanges of speech than in individual speech-acts. "Ideally," Nagel thinks the people in an exchange of speech should respond to someone's speech-embodied sense of self with "a contribution to his further embodiment which in turn enhances the original subject's sense of himself" (13). Like Grice, however, Nagel also recognizes the relevant "levels of mutual awareness" are achievable even with cutting speech which expresses "aggression." "If I am angry with someone I want to make him feel it, either to produce self-reproach . . . or to produce reciprocal anger or fear . . . a desire that the object of that anger be aroused" (12).

Like Nagel, Fingarette thinks a person's speech is most "distinctively human" when presented in exchanges with that of other people. But Fingarette also thinks an exchange of speech cannot be distinctively human unless it involves "reciprocal loyalty and respect" (1972/1998: 6–7). He thinks these features are "the general and fundamental requirements" of our being "'present' to each other" as humans (9). Beyond any initial feeling of embodiment in the illocutionary attitudes enacted by our utterances, that is, Fingarette thinks we must share reciprocal loyalty and respect in exchanges with other people if we are to feel relatively present with them as humans.[16] Such sharing would naturally facilitate superimposed, reflexive mutual recognition.

Perlocutionary Acts Are Not "Irresistible"
Even when our exchanges of speech do involve reciprocal loyalty and respect, Fingarette is significantly but helpfully wrong about a fourth sense in which our uses of speech can seem relatively effortless. This is the sense in which he suggests perlocutionary results then follow as effortlessly as do illocutionary ones when a given utterance is understood. In other words, Fingarette suggests the "power of a specific person to accomplish his will [in] directly and [relatively] effortlessly" concerns not just his illocutionary success but also his perlocutionary success. This, anyway, when he is perceived

as having reciprocal loyalty and respect, which Fingarette treats as "correct comportment" for Confucius.

> The magical element always involves great effects produced effortlessly, marvelously, with an irresistible power that is itself intangible, invisible, unmanifest. "With correct comportment, no commands are necessary, yet affairs proceed." (Fingarette, 1972/1998: 4, who quotes *Analects* 13: 6)

The perlocutionary effectiveness of a teacher perceived as having reciprocal loyalty and respect is illustrated in the responses of her professional acting students to Susan Batson.

> Part of the chemistry that exists between Batson and actors—"She can shake you like a tree and get the fruits down," Juliette Binoche says—comes from a sense of safety that her vigilance generates in them. . . . "She gives you confidence that when you go out there you know already you're good, because she said so." (Lahr, 2001: 93–94, whose second quote is from Jennifer Lopez)

In this example, a perlocutionary result follows relatively effortlessly because a speaker is perceived as having reciprocal loyalty and respect for an addressee. Nonetheless, this type of relative effortlessness is different from the first two types discussed above. We observed that a declaration of respect, for example, can be presented relatively effortlessly in the sense that a relevant fact follows deductively from listeners' understanding this utterance and the illocutionary attitude with which it is presented. This is true for both intentionalists and conventionalists, though they understand this fact's relationship to the truth of the correlative statement differently. Outside extralinguistic contexts, however, no perlocutionary result follows logically or deductively from our simply understanding an utterance.

In other words, affairs which might be commanded by some speaker within a certain extralinguistic context do not necessarily follow from our understanding her communicative intentions when expressed outside that extralinguistic context. Contrary to Fingarette's claim, not even those of our linguistic utterances that are fully understood have "an irresistible power" concerning their intended perlocutionary results. This is true even if, most typically, such results do follow from our being recognized as presenting utterances with reciprocal loyalty and respect. The inept suggestions by one of several friends lost in the wilderness, for example, are not irresistibly powerful no matter how much reciprocal loyalty and respect they involve. Fingarette's discussion of the natural magic within speech exchanges is thus flawed by not emphasizing this distinction between the relative effortlessness of using some utterance to create an illocutionary fact and that of using it to create the relevant perlocutionary result.[17]

No Single Speech-Act Completely Performs a Role

Fingarette's discussion is flawed in a related way that helps to explicate how anyone's use of speech-acts can be relatively effortless.

He rightly emphasizes that, when advancing a given utterance, speakers can focus either on the illocutionary act thus performed or on a role thus performed. Within the latter, however, we would focus on the utterance as part of ongoing acts related to being a respectful student, for example, not just on it as a single speech-act declaring respect. Fingarette observes it is obviously difficult to describe this type of relationship. On the one hand, no act seems always included by any role. On the other hand, no act seems always excluded by any role.[18] Regardless, there are many reasons why no single utterance can perform a role as completely as it can perform a single speech-act. Perhaps most generally, there is no formula outside extralinguistic contexts whereby one's role can be made explicit in the way "and that's a declaration of respect" makes "Thanks for being a wonderful teacher" an explicit declaration.

This extends a point raised by Turner in chapter 2: a friend's lie is different from that of a con artist even if their lie-expressing utterances are identical. In short, the illocutionary force of an utterance intended for role-expression depends on other acts. Whether or not someone's uttering "Thanks for being a wonderful teacher," for example, actually enacts a role of respectful student depends on how else she acts. This does not hold for the illocutionary force of that utterance considered as an individual speech-act, at least not when such force is made explicit and presented sincerely.

Thus, Fingarette is wrong to suggest that executing the role performed by some utterance is as effortless as is executing the individual speech-act that utterance performs. Fingarette should observe, for example, that being a lover in any significant sense involves many more acts than does a declaration of love. As a result, it is often more difficult to determine what counts as being a lover in various contexts than to determine what counts as being a declaration of love. Being a lover certainly requires more effort than does sincerely uttering "I declare my love for you."

Of course, the same is true of Fingarette's own example. Being a respectful student, involves many more acts than does a handshake, or saying "Thanks for being a wonderful teacher." As a result, it is often more difficult to determine what counts as being a respectful student in various contexts than to determine what counts as being a handshake, a promise, an excuse, a plea, or a compliment. Likewise, being a respectful student requires more effort than does sincerely declaring respect.

8. Criticisms of Conventionalism

This chapter has argued that speakers can feel embodied in speech-acts by focusing on the illocutionary attitudes thereby performed. We have also observed that conventionalists and intentionalists interpret this fact in different ways. As noted in chapter 3, however, most philosophers now regard intentionalism as the preferred interpretation of illocutionary acts. Neither space nor emphasis allows our addressing this fact adequately. Nonetheless, one of the most prominent intentionalistic criticisms has been implicitly answered in the discussion above.

Bach, for example, thinks conventionalists are wrong in treating any convention as adequate for explicitly capturing the myriad ways of performing a single illocutionary act.

> The variety of linguistic forms standardly used for the indirect performance of such speech-acts seems too open-ended to be explained by any convention (or set of conventions) that is supposed to specify just those linguistic forms whose utterance counts as the performance of an act of the relevant sort. (1998a: 303)

As observed above, however, Fingarette, Austin, and (perhaps) Searle have anticipated this challenge. In particular, Fingarette emphasizes that any device whose display counts as such a performance "alludes," either explicitly or tacitly, to some convention having the form: "Doing A in circumstance B counts also as doing C."

> In saying in the present context, "I apologize," I explicitly allude to the practice and thereby to its appropriate exercise in this situation by me. The allusion is explicit; but it need not be. I might make the allusion but make it tacitly. For example, I might only mention, using a conventional tone and manner (an "apologetic manner"), some crucial ground for my apologizing: "I'm very unhappy about it," or "I shouldn't have done it; it was unfair of me." (1967: 44)

In short, Fingarette appreciates that no convention with the above form is sufficiently broad as to explicitly identify just those ways in which we can implicitly perform a given illocutionary act. Because those ways involve many "subtle variations," Fingarette recognizes anyone's attempting to specify all of them would seem, at best, "quaint." His point is that a speaker can nonetheless use many implicit performative utterances in tacitly alluding to, fulfilling, the one convention governing some specific illoctutionary act. When it is understood, for example, saying "I declare my interest" counts also as a declaration, an illocutionary act, a new fact in the world. The same is true of "Gal, Ah'm crazy 'bout you." Their difference is that the former utterance alludes explicitly to the declaration-convention whereas the latter alludes tacitly. In Austin's terms, any implicit performative utterance is "conventional" in the sense that its illocutionary force "could be made explicit by the performative formula."

When illocutionary allusions are tacit, however, Fingarette agrees with Bach and Harnish that addressees can be wrong when identifying them. Just as for intentionalists, that is, conventionalistic addressees must defeasibly identify some unique illocutionary intention held by a speaker who presents some implicit performative utterance. For conventionalists, this is the intention to create a certain illocutionary fact in virtue of which the correlative statement becomes true. For intentionalists, it is the intention to present as true a statement that, when understood and accepted, creates a certain illocutionary fact. In each case, the identification by addressees is defeasible. But this is no more a problem for conventionalists than for intentionalists. Many implicit performative utterances simply resist addressees' knowing which unique illocutionary acts they are intended to perform.

A Second Criticism

A second criticism of conventionalism reverses the first one's strategy of emphasizing the variety of utterances with which we might perform a given illocutionary act. The second criticism emphasizes, instead, that a single (implicit, linguistic) utterance might perform several different illocutionary acts. Strawson (1964: 442, 444), for example, argues that "Don't go" might be uttered as a request, an order, or an entreaty. Indeed, it might be uttered as some combination of each, for which there is now no specific convention. Merely conjoining the normal conventions about requesting, ordering, and entreating would be inadequate for addressing this possibility. One conjunction, after all, could emphasize one element to a certain extent while others could emphasize that element to a variety of other extents. Since "Don't go" clearly makes sense without a specific convention in this case, however, Strawson thinks it makes sense in every case. Conventions, that is, are superfluous in understanding any illocutionary act of the implicit, linguistic type.

While Strawson (442) recognizes Austin's insight that implicit performatives can be made explicit by the performative formula whenever this becomes useful, his argument does not fully engage the insight. Conventionalists, however, do suggest only that we can identify explicit behavioral criteria for any specific illocutionary purpose associated with a single implicit performative whenever this becomes useful. If it becomes useful to identify some specific combination of requesting, ordering, and entreating when uttering "Don't go," for example, we will develop behavioral criteria for thus presenting this utterance. Such criteria might involve a specific tone and rhythm with which to issue the utterance. Alternatively, they might involve some neologism designating the relevant combination of requesting, ordering, and entreating. Uttering "Don't go" with these devices would then be different from uttering it without them.

Implicitly, at least, Strawson's explication of P-predicates seems to endorse our ability to associate a neologism with specific behavioral criteria even if that involves some specific illocutionary state of mind.

> [I]n the case of at least some P-predicates, the ways of telling [whether a given individual "possesses" the type of "consciousness" relevant to a certain combination of requesting, ordering and entreating] must constitute in some sense logically adequate kinds of criteria for the ascription of the P-predicate. (1959/1963: 102)

In the absence of such specific criteria, on the other hand, we simply cannot know precisely what a speaker intends by uttering "Don't go." This does not, however, mean the above conventions would be superfluous concerning the illocutionary act thereby performed. It means only that we do not know precisely how they should be combined with one another. Hence, we do not know precisely what illocutionary act someone's uttering "Don't go" performs.

On the other hand, this problem is not repaired by construing "Don't go" intentionalistically in the manner of Bach and Harnish. Indeed, it is exacerbated. Unlike conventionalists, after all, intentionalists such as Bach and Harnish regard as defeasible even the inference from an unambiguous explicit linguistic performative to a speaker's illocutionary attitude.

9. Summary and Projections

Without further discussion, let us assume that communicatively successful speech-acts can be interpreted conventionalistically as well as intentionalistically. In either case, there are several senses in which they can produce "further results."

Most simply, they can create new illocutionary facts in the world as associated with correlative statements as true, though conventionalists and intentionalists disagree about the logical priority between these two creations. By attending to such creations, we can be self-aware in some specific way, the way in which an illocutionary attitude (of demanding or questioning, for example) seems embodied in a given speech-act.

When a speech-act is an implicit performative, listeners must regard their understanding of its illocutionary force as defeasible regardless of whether they employ a conventionalistic or an intentionalistic interpretation of that speech-act. When it is an explicit performative, both conventionalists and intentionalists think it is easier to identify the illocutionary force of a speech-act. It is therefore relatively easy for listeners to recognize appropriate perlocutionary responses to speech-acts that are explicitly performative. Except in extralinguistic contexts, however, perlocutionary results do not follow so automatically as do illocutionary ones when a speech-act is understood. This is true even when everyone involved has reciprocal loyalty and respect. On the other hand, these features obviously facilitate exchanges of speech-acts that involve the type of depth Nagel recommends—namely, superimposed, reflexive, and mutual recognition of each person as embodied in her or his speech-acts.

For both conventionalists and intentionalists, successful communication requires illocutionary success. It therefore invites a speaker's self-awareness to be identified with her illocutionary attitudes as embodied in her speech-acts. Among those who are professional, this has more relevance for presentational than for representational actors. After all, it is important for the former but not for the latter that one's speech-acts embody some emotion or sense of self. No doubt, there are many ways on- and offstage in which this might be accomplished. The debate between conventionalists and intentionalists specifies one of these—namely, the illocutionary attitudes embodied in a person's speech-acts literally can be her felt senses of self. As observed regarding Magee's list of implicit performatives, such an attitude is not just, say, a demand or a question in general. Rather, it is a specific type of question, a playfully jesting one for example: "So you as sweet as all that?"

Speakers with affective energy are different from those who are presentational, though both can focus on their illocutionary attitudes. A presentational speaker can focus on her illocutionary attitudes to "make one's self seen and heard" for the purpose of communicating effectively with listeners. A speaker with affective energy, on the other hand, can focus on her illocutionary attitudes primarily to enhance various senses of self for herself.

In an exchange of speech-acts, a speaker's affective energy can be used internalistically or externalistically. Under the former, it is used to support some satisfying sense of self for a speaker. Under the latter, it is used to fulfill the conditions other people seem to associate with certain roles. Both uses can but need not be fulfilled at once, and both can be fulfilled with conventionalistically as well as with intentionalistically interpreted speech-acts. However, intentionalistically interpreted speech-acts provide a speaker with more self-control than do conventionalistically interpreted speech-acts. The reason is that, regardless of its communicative success, a speaker can regard as true the statement associated with a given illocutionary speech-act only when this is interpreted intentionalistically.

Chapter 5 uses these concepts in analyzing some of the speech-acts of Janie Crawford as she evolves from child to matriarch. It will do so by considering the argument of Henry Louis Gates, Jr. that Janie develops what W. E. B. Du Bois described as double-consciousness. This will illustrate Janie's using affective energy to speak internalistically.

Notes

1. On the one hand, Fingarette agrees with Searle that, when understood in appropriate contexts, our satisfying certain linguistic conventions suffices for our performing certain further acts. "[T]he further act 'brought about' [by uttering 'I apologize'] is . . . a purely 'logical' consequence of an accepted rule or convention of the form 'Doing A in circumstance B counts also as doing C'" (1967: 44). On the other hand, Fingarette agrees with Searle that our satisfying such conventions is necessary for this. Such "language cannot be understood in isolation from the conventional practice in which it is rooted" (1972/1998: 14).

2. Searle recognizes that an utterance's success as an efficient cause need not involve its communicative success. This occurs, for example, if "somebody rigs up a transducer device sensitive to acoustic signals which is such that if he stands next to his car and says 'I hereby start the car,' the car will start" (1989: 550, note 11).

There are nonetheless two reasons why communicative success does seem involved by Searle's supernatural example. First, the example is introduced as an exception to what he thinks is a general feature of declarations that change extralinguistic facts about the world. "The most prominent exceptions to the claim that [extralinguistic] declarations require an extralinguistic institution are supernatural declarations" (1989: 549). Second, Searle also thinks any declaration's success "requires recognition by the audience" (548). It thus seems there is a sense in which Searle thinks his supernatural example does involve communicative success. In contrast, the transducer example involves an utterance that is "obviously not" a declaration at all.

3. As observed in chapter 1, on the other hand, the supernatural concept of magic for traditional Africans concerns speech as sometimes necessary, but never as sufficient, for certain physical changes.

4. Fingarette recognizes we might seem "quaint and extreme" when specifying the conventions relevant to any social practice. Nonetheless, he thinks some such specifying is useful in demonstrating their complexity. After all, there are "indescribably many subtleties in the distinctions, nuances and minute but meaningful variations in gesture" (1972/1998: 10) of relevance to even a single convention.

5. As discussed in the next section, Fingarette most obviously thinks an utterance, in particular, is effortless in the sense that, as understood, it constitutes a certain "further act." Here, then, it seems more appropriate for him to treat magic as the power, derived from certain utterance-containing rituals, to accomplish one's will effortlessly but indirectly concerning such further acts.

6. Searle's discussion in note 2 of chapter 3 above suggests the same point: "every declaration that is not a performative could have been one" if employed with an appropriate "performative expression." Austin (1962: 103) also suggests the same point, that any utterance is "*conventional* in the sense that at least it[s illocutionary force] could be made explicit by the performative formula." With respect to Fingarette's illustration in the text, for example, the illocutionary force to which someone's uttering "I'm very unhappy about it" might allude implicitly could be made explicit by her instead uttering "I apologize."

7. Fingarette prefers Austin's initial distinction between performative and constative utterances to his later one among the locutionary, illocutionary, and perlocutionary acts performed by a single utterance. Austin (1962: 55), of course, rejected the former distinction because he found that many utterances satisfy not only the best criteria he could develop for performatives but also those for constatives. In contrast, Fingarette thinks "the same expression or sentence *may* be simultaneously used in different ways" (1972/1998: 47, emphasis added). For example, "'I warn you . . .' suggests the performative, and '. . . the bull is about to charge' suggests the constative" (1972/1998: 47).

Fingarette's type of concern actually seems anticipated by Austin's replacing his initial distinction with his later one.

> With the constative utterance, we abstract from the illocutionary (let alone the perlocutionary) aspects of the speech-act, and we concentrate on the locutionary. . . . With the performative utterance, we attend as much as possible to the illocutionary force of the utterance. . . . The doctrine of the performative/constative distinction stands to the doctrine of locutionary and illocutionary acts in the total speech-act as the *special* theory to the *general* theory. (1962: 145–46, 148)

8. It is noteworthy that Strawson (1959/1963) denies this. He does so while explicating his concept of P-predicates, such as "'believes in God'" (100), predicates which "imply the possession of consciousness on the part of that to which they are ascribed" (101). According to Strawson,

> one ascribes P-predicates to others on the strength of observation of their behaviour. . . . [T]he behaviour-criteria one goes on are not just signs of the presence of what is

meant by the P-predicate, but are criteria of a logically adequate kind for the ascription of the P-predicate. (102–103)

Presumably, a person's uttering "I believe in God" is one such item of behavior. Apparently, then, Strawson thinks our inferring from this utterance to someone's having truly stated her belief in God (and, no doubt, other behavior satisfying other relevant criteria) is logically adequate, not defeasible.

9. This is true, anyway, of conventionalists such as Fingarette who are explicitly concerned with implicit performatives, speech that alludes "tacitly" to the conventions in terms of which facts are produced by such speech. The case is not so clear concerning Searle. As observed in note 6, on the one hand, Searle thinks any implicit performative (such as "'I intend to come'") can be made explicit if employed with an appropriate performative expression. On the other hand, Searle explicitly denies his interest in implicit performatives. "On my usage, the only performatives are what Austin called 'explicit performatives'" (1989: 536). Indeed, Searle seems to interpret implicit performatives as do intentionalists. "If I say, 'I intend to come,' I have literally just made a statement about my intention. (Though, of course, in making such a statement, I might also indirectly be making a promise" [1989: 536].)

10. Of course, few intentionalists regard the truth of whatever statement is associated with an utterance as being entirely independent of other people's understandings. Intentionalists do not accept this even for utterances that are implicitly performative so as to focus on a speaker. Strawson (1959/1963) provides a prominent reason concerning P-predicates.

[I]t is essential to the character of these predicates that they have both first- and third-person ascriptive uses, that they are both self-ascribable otherwise than on the basis of observation of the behaviour of the subject of them, and other-ascribable on the basis of behaviour criteria. (104)

Strawson illustrates this view with the example of "feeling depressed." "X's depression *is* something, one and the same thing, which is felt, but not observed, by X, and observed, but not felt, by others than X" (105). Thus, for normal people anyway, our self-ascriptions are inevitably influenced by the other-ascriptions of other people. This is true even of utterances that are self-ascriptive in virtue of being implicitly performative, as when one regards herself as asking when uttering "I really want you to go."

The point in the text is thus a relative one. Intentionalists focus on a performative utterance as presenting a true statement and thereby, when understood, as creating a new fact. In contrast, conventionalists focus on a performative utterance, when understood, as creating a new fact and thereby as grounding the truth of that utterance's propositional content. Relatively speaking, then, the truth of an implicit performative is less dependent on other people's understanding for intentionalistic speakers than it is for conventionalistic ones.

11. There is no standard nomenclature for designating the traditional/newer contrast in acting methods. When designating this contrast in her (1991), for example, Hagen shifts from the Representational/Presentational distinction to one between formalism and realism. On the other hand, Grotowski (1995), who founded the innovative Polish Laboratory Theater, always uses "presentation" in designating the traditional method. The newer approach when considered alone is, of course, often organized as what is called the Method. For convenience in designating the contrast between the traditional approach and the newer one, let us continue using "representational" and "presentational" as above.

12. The sense in which presentationalists "ignore the audience" is therefore limited. Presentationalists do tend to ignore inflections and poses they think might affect audiences concerning the interpretation of a performance. On the other hand, presentationalists do not ignore audiences altogether. Rather, they focus primarily on expressing their subjective experiences in "true" ways; but they do this so as to make themselves "heard and seen" by audiences.

13. Ramblin' Jack Elliott, folk singer and raconteur, makes the same point about Woody Guthrie, the very early Bob Dylan, and himself. "Dylan learned from me the same way I learned from Woody. Woody didn't teach me. He just said, 'If you want to learn something, just steal it—that's the way I learned from Lead Belly'" (as quoted by Coburn, 1984: 85).

14. Even Olivier recognizes that the presentational approach is communicatively effective for some people.

> The first morning made my heart sink, a sensation I was getting profoundly sick of; we had spent the whole time trying to inject a scintillating spirit into the scene of our first meeting [with Marilyn Monroe, who was to co-star with and be directed by Olivier in *The Prince and the Showgirl*]. I had never dreamed up such a variety of expressions, examples, illustrations, images to help inspire the essential wit and sparkle needed to make a livelier start to a picture from which a great deal would be expected. Marilyn made her inevitable way towards Paula [Strasberg], who said, "Honey, just think of Coca-Cola and Frankie Sinatra!" I suppose that might have been the Actors Studio approach [established by Paula's husband Lee, among others]. God! Don't tell me they would have been right and I wrong throughout this whole thing? Needless to say, it worked; enough to make a man cut his throat, enough for this man, anyway. (1982: 211)

15. Siebel (352) relies on personal communication with Bach in thus explicating "the *basic idea*" Bach shares with Harnish: "a necessary and sufficient condition for performing these [illocutionary] acts is to express mental states."

16. Given its importance for his view of Confucian magic, Fingarette's discussion of reciprocal loyalty and respect is unfortunately thin. In several passages (9, 10, 42), however, his discussion employs "reciprocal good faith and respect" rather than "reciprocal loyalty and respect." The former usage might be helpfully seen as involving William James's (1897/1960) well-known concept of preliminary faith.

James observes there are many "cases [of 'personal relations, states of mind between one man and another'] where a fact cannot come at all unless a preliminary faith exists in its coming" (25). In other words, James maintains the existence of such facts requires someone's having had "active faith" or "active good-will" or "precursive faith" that her addressee would responsively participate in kind to performances embodying those states of mind. According to James, active good-will is "meeting the hypothesis half-way." Among his many examples, one person's "liking" another is perhaps most relevant to Fingarette's discussion. "Whether you do or not depends, in countless instances, on whether I meet you half-way, am willing to assume that you must like me, and show you trust and expectations" (23). Like Fingarette, James also emphasizes the need for precursive faith within institutions such as a "government, an army, a commercial system, a ship, a college, an athletic team."

Perhaps, then, Fingarette can be helpfully seen as thinking we feel unusually present when speaking with one another if our speech exhibits preliminary faith in mutual respect and is well received.

17. Though he agrees with some of the "underlying spirit" in Fingarette's discussion, Loy (2002: 202) also agrees with us that Fingarette's "examples of handshaking and making a request are not very convincing as non-trivial examples of magic." In particular, Loy agrees that perlocutionary effects do not follow irresistibly from illocutionary understandings in linguistic contexts. Indeed, Loy observes this is true even in extralinguistic contexts. Some urgent demand from outside such a context, after all, might suddenly remove one or more addressees from that context.

18. Fingarette's example of always being warmly reserved when shaking hands with a respected teacher ignores a student's role with teachers who deny that respect involves subordination, for example, or with those who celebrate successes robustly. Likewise, his example of never slapping a respected teacher on the back ignores a student's role with teachers on a departmental softball team.

CHAPTER FIVE

Speech and Senses of Self in *Their Eyes Were Watching God*

1. Three Types of Discourse

Magee (1999) observes of professional drama that "the amount of 'action' a play is felt to contain depends on the nature and distribution within it of different sorts of speech-act" (120). In large measure, a similar observation can be true of how one views her own senses of self—it can depend on the nature and distribution of different sorts of her speech-acts. It can depend, in particular, on the illocutionary attitudes she intends to express. These can constitute her speech-embodied senses of self, as considered in chapters 3 and 4. We now expand the point by considering the evolution in Janie Crawford's speech-embodied senses of self.

Gates (1988) observes that a large proportion of the speech-acts associated with Janie are delivered in what is called free indirect discourse. Thus, any discussion of Janie's speech-embodied senses of self must first consider this fascinating form of speech, as we now do by addressing Gates's argument. In doing so, we also examine Gates's using Du Bois's concept of double-consciousness to analyze Janie's senses of self.

Free Indirect Discourse
Gates thinks Hurston literally reshaped the debate about how to address Black dialect without thereby suggesting "[b]lack innate mental inferiority" (176). According to Gates, Hurston's primary technique in this regard is her use of free indirect discourse—discourse that is contrasted not only with direct discourse but also with indirect discourse.

Gates observes that direct discourse in *Their Eyes* is "always foregrounded by quotation marks and by its Black diction" (191), and presents a character's words as said by him or her. Indirect discourse, on the other hand, never appears within quotation marks. Rather, "its signals of time and person correspond to a third-person narrator's discourse" (208), discourse in which "one source would be describing another" (210). Gates (209) illustrates this type with Janie's contemplating her pear tree revelation, which is considered further below: "The vision of Logan Killicks was desecrating the pear tree, but Janie didn't know how to tell Nanny that" (Hurston, 1937/1998: 14).

For Gates, free indirect discourse is "a third or mediating term between narrative commentary and direct discourse" (191) which he finds exemplified primarily by a passage in which Joe Starks announces himself to Janie.

> He had always wanted to be a big voice, but de white folks had all de sayso where he come from and everywhere else, exceptin' dis place dat colored folks was buildin' theirselves.[1] Dat was right too. De man dat built things oughta boss it. (Hurston, 1937/1998: 28)

Here, Gates notes direct and indirect discourses are "blended" or "merged" into a "double-voiced utterance, in which two voices co-occur" (209). On the one hand, "the assertion originates within and reflects the character's sensibilities, not the narrator's" (210). On the other hand, it appears in the third person. "There are no quotation marks here . . . this is an account of the words that Joe spoke to Janie" (210). Gates concludes there is "a fusion of narrator and a silent but speaking character" (210) to yield "represented discourse" (191).

When applying this concept to "Jane Austen's fictions," Gates describes it as "narrative-cum-dialogue." Typically, of course, the fusion within free indirect discourse represents both the narrator's discourse and that of a single character. Gates observes, however, that "Hurston uses free indirect discourse not only to represent an individual character's speech and thought but also to represent the collective Black community's speech and thoughts" (214). His example comes from a scene just before a devastating hurricane. "Most of the great flame-throwers were there and naturally, handling Big John de Conquer and his works. How he had done everything big on earth, then went up tuh heben without dying atall" (Hurston, 1937/1998: 156–57).

Gates's most general observation is that

> free indirect discourse attempts to represent "consciousness without the apparent intrusion of a narrative voice," thereby "presenting the illusion of a

character's acting out his [or her] mental state in an immediate relationship with the reader."[2]

Within free indirect discourse, that is, Gates thinks readers are as immediately confronted by a character as are his or her addressees. We are introduced to Joe Starks, for example, by free indirect discourse apparently directed to us, as readers, as much as to Janie. Gates thinks this strengthens our illusion of Joe's acting out his mental state relatively immediately.

2. Free Indirect Discourse, Double-Consciousness, and Self-Control

According to Gates, the free indirect discourse associated with all Black characters in *Their Eyes*, except Janie, involves a single type of diction: dialect. In contrast, Gates describes two types of diction in the free indirect discourse associated with Janie, neither of which is dialect.

Initially, this diction is that of standard English, which Gates illustrates with Janie's reflecting on having experienced "the longing for love, and then her first orgasm" (210) while lying under the blooming pear tree considered above.[3] "Oh to be a pear tree—*any* tree in bloom! With kissing bees singing of the beginning of the world! She was sixteen" (Hurston, 1937/1998: 11). Gates concludes "the narrator is interpreting Janie's inarticulate thoughts to the reader on her behalf" (211), but with a diction (standard) different from that of Janie's direct speech (dialect).

Much later, after Janie begins to challenge Joe's authority "if only in her thoughts," however, Gates generalizes that the diction of the free indirect discourse associated with her "more and more" ceases to be standard. "Janie's free indirect discourse . . . is represented in an idiom informed by the Black idiom but translated into what we might think of as a colloquial form of standard English which always stands in contrast to Janie's direct speech, which is foregrounded in dialect" (211).

Gates provides no further explicit discussion of the distinction between dialect and colloquial standard dictions. From the example immediately below and from others he considers (212, 214), however, we can draw the following conclusion. Colloquial standard diction contains some items of dialect but proportionately fewer than those in the self-announcement associated with Joe above. As considered in section 3 below, the vagueness of this explication raises one of several problems for Gates's argument, in which colloquial standard diction is illustrated with the following passage. "But then when Lige or Sam or Walter or some of the other big picture talkers were using a side of the world for a canvas, Joe would hustle her off inside the store to see something. Look like he took pleasure in doing it. Why couldn't he go himself sometimes?" (Hurston, 1937/1998: 54).

Gates thinks there is a significant result from this difference between the diction of Janie's direct discourse (dialect) and that of the free indirect discourse (colloquial standard) often associated with her after she begins to explicitly challenge Joe's authority. Specifically, Gates thinks this difference indicates she has a type of "double-consciousness," of which she is not yet aware, quite analogous to that discussed by Du Bois.[4] When Janie later begins lying to herself about Joe's significance, considered in chapter 2 above, Gates thinks she becomes aware of this "apparently exhilarating double-consciousness" and of her ability to "move the parts simultaneously through contiguous spaces." "It was like a drug. In a way it was good because it reconciled her to things. She got so she received all things with the stolidness of the earth which soaks up urine and perfume with the same indifference" (Hurston, 1937/1998: 77). According to Gates, this is the "crucial event that [eventually] enables her to speak and assert herself" (204).

Despite the dogged strength involved by Du Bois's sense of double-consciousness, that is, Gates (204) thinks Janie's can be exhilarating. He finds this interpretation supported by Hurston's linking images of prostration and relaxation with an image concerning lonesomeness and summertime, and delivered in free indirect discourse.

> Then one day she sat and watched the shadow of herself going about tending the store and prostrating itself before Jody, while all the time she herself sat under a shady tree with the wind blowing through her hair and her clothes. Somebody near about making summertime out of lonesomeness. (1937/1998: 77)

Gates also thinks Janie's double-consciousness eventually allows her to modify the way she has previously expressed the merger of her senses of self—presumably, those just considered, one as prostrated and one as relaxed. Eventually, that is, Janie thrice explicitly challenges Joe before he dies, thereby "coming to consciousness" with "self-discovery" of "her authority" (202, 203).[5] Nonetheless, Gates emphasizes the diction of Janie's direct discourse (dialect) remains different from that of the free indirect discourse associated with her (colloquial standard). He therefore denies that Janie's discovering her authority over her double-consciousness ever yields a "unified identity" for her. Relying on certain generalizations about the diction of the narrator's indirect discourse, Gates instead affirms Janie and eventually gains "a maximum of self-control over the division. . . . [This] is the novel's sign of Janie's synthesis" (213–14). Specifically, the fact that the dialect of Janie's direct discourse finally "colors" the narrator's own idiom confirms her having, indeed, gained such synthesis. At the conclusion of the novel, that is, "the narrator's idiom [colloquial standard] . . . resembles rather closely the idiom in which Janie's free indirect discourse is [now] rendered [colloquial standard]" (214).

3. Gates's Argument Is Helpful but Flawed

Gates's argument is helpful in at least two respects. Perhaps most simply, it is interesting to consider his suggestion that Hurston's use of free indirect discourse enhances an illusion. For Gates, this is the illusion of a character's acting out his or her mental states relatively immediately with readers. Presumably, on the other hand, such illusions are relative to individual readers. For me, the illusion most strengthened by the free indirect discourse associated with a Hurston-character is that of sharing consciousness with the source of such discourse. The third-person merged with a character in free indirect discourse seems to me to be me, in other words, not the narrator. Let us explore this issue no further, however.

More importantly, Gates seems right that Janie's relationship with Joe sometimes involves examples of double-consciousness interestingly and significantly analogous to the type identified by Du Bois. "She had an inside and an outside now and suddenly she knew how not to mix them" (Hurston, 1937/1998: 72). In particular, the examples of double-consciousness concerning Janie involve two "unreconciled" senses of self, only one of which is endorsed by prevailing social authority.

Three Flaws in Gates's Argument

Nonetheless, there are three reasons why Gates does not seem justified in maintaining about Janie that "consciousness of her own division" is "expressed in free indirect discourse" (208) as this is associated with her.

The first is a conceptual problem: Gates's treatment of free indirect discourse is ambiguous. As exemplified by the following claim, he sometimes treats the free indirect discourse associated with Janie as something that is exclusively hers. "Almost never, however, curiously enough, does Janie's free indirect discourse unfold in a strictly Black idiom, as does Joe's" (211). At other times, however, Gates treats the free indirect discourse associated with

Janie as something that is not possessed exclusively by her, but instead belongs to "a fusion" involving her and the narrator. Indeed, Gates sometimes treats this fusion as itself "a hybrid character" whose speech "is not the voice of both a character and a narrator . . . but a blend of both" (209, xxv). At still other times, as we have seen, Gates treats this fusion as "the narrator is interpreting Janie's inarticulate thoughts to the reader on her behalf" (211). (Free indirect discourse would here fail in what Gates identifies as its general function of representing "consciousness without the apparent intrusion of a narrative voice.")

The second problem facing Gates's argument concerns his view that colloquial standard is the form of the free indirect discourse associated with Janie after she begins challenging Joe's authority in her thoughts. In fact, this diction is often standard rather than colloquial standard.

> Sometimes Janie would think of the old days in the big white house and the store and laugh to herself. What if Eatonville could see her now in her blue denim overalls and heavy shoes? The crowd of people around her and a dice game on her floor! (Hurston, 1937/1998: 134)

On the other hand, the diction of the free indirect discourse then associated with Janie occasionally duplicates the dialect of her direct discourse.

> But oh God, don't let Tea Cake be off somewhere hurt and Ah not know nothing about it. And God, please suh, don't let him love nobody else but me. Maybe Ah'm is uh fool, Lawd, lak dey say, but Lawd, Ah been so lonesome, and Ah been waitin', Jesus. Ah done waited uh long time. (120)

At most, then, the direct/free diction-difference associated with Janie might indicate a double-consciousness for her slightly more than the correlative differences do for other characters.

But such an indication is relatively insignificant when considered against the fact that many characters other than Janie are equally associated with "the double-voiced nature of free indirect discourse." As observed above, for example, Gates himself indicates that free indirect discourse is associated with everyone in "the collective Black community." Furthermore, when generalizing about the free indirect discourse of a single individual Gates observes "The character's idiom . . . [is then] interspersed and contrasted colorfully with the narrator's voice" (210). This involves the clearest sense of double-consciousness associated with free indirect discourse considered by Gates. Such consciousness belongs to a hybrid blend of two elements, and is associated with many characters as much as with Janie. In this case, however, free indirect discourse does not serve Gates's purpose of explaining what he thinks is unique about Janie.

The third problem facing Gates's argument concerns his explicating the supposed uniqueness of the dictions of free indirect discourse associated with Janie. According to this explication, the dictions of the free indirect discourse associated with Janie (standard and colloquial standard) are unique in "almost never" being the same as that of her direct discourse (dialect).

But this assumption of uniqueness is false, especially as concerns Joe. On the one hand, the diction of the free indirect discourse associated with Joe is sometimes different from the dialect of his direct discourse in virtue of being standard English.

> On the train the next day, Joe didn't make many speeches with rhymes to her, but he bought her the best things the butcher had, like apples and a glass lantern full of candies. Mostly he talked about plans for the town when he got there. They were bound to need somebody like him. (34)

Indeed, even the free indirect discourse associated with a group can involve diction that is standard rather than the dialect of the group's direct discourse. This is exemplified by Janie's suitors after Joe's death, who "felt that it was not fitting to mention desire to the widow of Joseph Starks. You spoke of honor and respect" (93).

On the other hand, the diction of the free indirect discourse associated with Joe is often different from the dialect of his direct discourse in virtue of being colloquial standard. As mentioned above, Gates's discussion leaves this difference vague, for it does not specify proportionately how much of a passage's diction must be dialect before it ceases it be colloquial standard. Clearly, however, the proportion of dialect-items in the following passage containing free indirect discourse associated with Joe is substantially less than the correlative proportion in the self-announcement associated with him above.

> Here he was just pouring honor all over her; building a high chair for her to sit in and overlook the world and she here pouting over it! Not that he wanted anybody else, but just too many women would be glad to be in her place. (62)

Indeed, colloquial standard diction appears in the free indirect discourse associated with characters other than Joe or Janie.

Just before day the party wore out. So Tea Cake hurried on back to his new wife. He had done found out how rich people feel and he had a fine guitar and twelve dollars left in his pocket and all he needed now was a great big old hug and kiss from Janie. (124)

Janie as Herself as Well as the Narrator

In sum, Gates is wrong to assume there is a relationship that is clear, significant, and unique concerning the diction of Janie's direct discourse and those of the free indirect discourses associated with her. As we shall continue to discuss, Gates is right to emphasize Janie sometimes has a type of double-consciousness comparable to that identified by Du Bois. Still, Gates is wrong to explore this with his analysis of free indirect discourse. As Hurston uses it, of course, this technique remains interesting. Perhaps it strengthens the illusion of a character's acting out his or her mental state relatively immediately. Perhaps it strengthens the illusion of our sharing consciousness with a character. Regardless, Hurston employs the technique in several ways, and she does so not only with Janie but also with many other characters. No clear and significant relationship emerges that uniquely involves Janie.

It might seem that Janie, and only Janie, narrates practically all of *Their Eyes*. The reason is that "while Janie talked" (7) describes its source, and "'Now dat's how everything wuz, Pheoby, jus' lak Ah told yuh'" (191) concludes its presentation. Gates might thus use this apparently unique relationship between the narrator and Janie to develop his thesis relating the diction of her discourse to that of the free indirect discourse associated with her, a discourse he would think involves the narrator (Janie) as well as a character (Janie). Such a development, however, would render as even less clear the various "fusion[s] of narrator and a silent but speaking character" when we consider not only Janie but also Nanny, Joe, and Tea Cake as characters. Besides, Gates himself implicitly rejects this type of development: "the bracketed tale, in the novel, is told by an omniscient, third-person narrator who reports thoughts, feelings, and events that Janie could not possibly have heard or seen" (1988: 196)—the buzzards' conversation after the funeral of Matt Bonner's mule, for example (Hurston, 1937/1998: 61–62).

In any case, much of what we know about Janie is presented in the free indirect discourse associated with her. It cannot be ignored in any discussion of her senses of self concerned with how they might be embodied in speech. So far as I know, all sides agree that Janie should be regarded as one source of this discourse. For now, then, let us ignore how the other source of such merged discourse should be interpreted. Instead, let us seek the most obvious explanation for how Janie's senses of self might be embodied not only in that type of discourse but also in her direct discourse.

4. Changes in Janie's Sense of Self before "She Became a Woman"

Even before Janie becomes "a woman," her sense of self has undergone three significant changes. Analyzing these helps to clarify those that occur thereafter, our primary concern.

At age six, Janie discovers she is not white by seeing a photograph of her four playmates and herself. While initially disconcerted ("'Aw, aw! Ah'm colored!'" [9]), Janie continues "havin' fun" with these children, their mother, and their grandparents, the Washburns, who employ Nanny and help to raise Janie while Nanny helps to raise their four grandchildren. Apparently, no double-consciousness results in the manner specified by Du Bois above, in which one existing sense of self feels pity or contempt for another. Rather, an old sense of self is knowingly and self-respectfully replaced by a new sense, a point better expressed with a distinction introduced in chapter 1.

Like anyone's, Janie's "externalistic" sense of self intends to fulfill the conditions she thinks apt for other people's identifying her as enacting certain roles—those of friend or of cook's helper, for example. Though Janie has just learned to eliminate one element from any convincing role, this has occurred before it must inhibit any of her "internalistic" senses of self. These are those embodied in acts that seem satisfying to her—those in sharing food or in preparing it, for example. After all, no one she knows then responds differently to these acts she now performs as "colored."

Janie therefore can and does continue to perform acts at the Washburn's that not only fall within the range of now accessible roles but also feel satisfying. Such self-control need not involve double-consciousness in any of the senses specified by Du Bois above. It certainly need not involve feelings of self-pity or of self-contempt. Nor need it involve strivings that feel unreconciled with each other. It need only involve a continuing choice to find self-embodying acts that actually feel satisfying within the constraints imposed by accessible roles. So long as this is possible, Janie can avoid unreconciled senses of self roughly as Hurston reports about herself.

> I saw thirty-odd people [in a traveling Gilbert and Sullivan troupe Hurston joined as a teen] made up of all classes and races living a communal life. There were little touches of professional jealousy and a catty crack now and then, but

let sickness or trouble touch any member and the whole cast rallied around to help out. . . . With all branches of Anglo-Saxon, Irish, three Jews and one Negro together in a huddle, and all friendly, there were a lot of racial gags. Everybody was so sure that nobody hesitated to pull them. . . . [T]he whole experience on that job gave me an approach to racial understanding. It was easy to keep on feeling that way. . . . I had been privileged to see folks substituting love for failure of career. . . . I had seen careers filling up the empty holes left by love. . . . Working with these people I had been sitting by a warm fire for a year and a half and gotten used to the feel of peace. (1942/1996: 117–19)

For Hurston, the roles available within an all-Black community are replaced by those available within a broadly diverse one; but the new roles provide access to self-embodying acts that are satisfying. For Janie, the roles available to a young White girl on the Washburn property are replaced by those available to a young Black girl there. By providing access to self-embodying acts that are satisfying, however, the new roles provide access to satisfying senses of self.

A similar result follows the second change in Janie's externalistic senses of self. Schoolmates tease her until she and Nanny move away from the Washburn property. Broad social acceptance, that is, requires Janie's eliminating certain behavior involving the Washburns, which she apparently accepts with equanimity. These new constraints on her externalistic senses of self, that is, allow Janie's continued access to self-embodying acts which feel satisfying. She still does not have double-consciousness. The acts she performs to enact her new community-based role embody satisfying senses of self. Thus, when Janie later ponders her future as a rich widow following Joe's death, she considers returning to "the old stomping ground" (89). But she does so to focus on her lost mother and on Nanny's grave, with no attention at all to the Washburns. Janie's sense of being White, or of living with Whites, has simply been replaced with other senses, ones involving self-embodying acts that are satisfying.

Janie's Sense of Self Changes with Logan Killicks

Janie's third change is more complex and more inhibiting. After the pear-tree-revelation awakens Janie's sexuality, Nanny insists she is a marriageable woman. Though disconcerted ("'Naw, Nanny, naw Ah ain't no real 'oman yet'" [12]), Janie agrees to marry wealth, trusting Nanny that "she would love Logan after they were married" (21). Shortly, however, Janie views Logan's house as "absent of flavor" and him as old, fat, unattractive, dirty, and smelly. Although Logan is a hard worker, he pays less and less attention to Janie as an equally significant person with thoughts, desires, and emotions. After a year, she "knew now that marriage did not make love. Janie's first dream was dead, so she became a woman" (25).[6]

Janie nonetheless refuses to perform several of the acts typically associated with wives in her community. For example, Janie refuses to chop and fetch into the house wood already cut by Logan and delivered to the house; or to fetch water; or to help clean the barn. To this extent, her externalistic sense of self as Logan's wife does not force her into self-embodying acts she finds unsatisfying. On the other hand, the self-embodying acts identified by her pear-tree-revelation do not seem satisfying when performed with Logan. "'But Nanny, Ah wants to want him sometimes. Ah don't want him to do all de wantin'" (23). Janie's socially endorsed externalistic sense of self as Logan's wife thus seems linked to a sense of self related to pity. Her externalistic sense of self is certainly unreconciled with her sense of self as focused on acts of love and sex. "She had been getting ready for her great journey to the horizons in search of *people*.... But she had been whipped like a cur dog, and run off down a back road after *things*" (89). To this extent, Janie has double-consciousness in a manner similar to that specified by Du Bois.

What is interesting is that Janie avoids such double-consciousness relatively easily after deciding, a year into marriage, that "familiar people and things had failed her" (25). In other words, Janie's sense of self-control has not become dependent on a Logan- or Nanny-centered sense of self. When given the opportunity, rather, she "ran to the pump" and implicitly invited conversation with "a cityfied, stylish dressed man," Joe Starks, a dozen years her senior, who "talked friendly" and who spoke of "far horizon" as well as "change and chance" (29). After Logan later threatens to beat her for a different matter, Janie leaves with Joe. "From now on until death she was going to have flower dust and springtime sprinkled over everything" (32). Minimally, this free indirect discourse indicates Janie's believing her externalistic sense of self as Joe's wife will feel reconciled with her sense of self as struggling for love, sex, and personal answers in life. In particular, the speech enacting her externalistic sense of self as his wife will, she believes, also be self-embodying acts of love, sex, and answer-questing which feel satisfying, which enhance her internalistic sense of self as satisfied.

5. Changes in Janie's Speech and Sense of Self with Joe

As a woman, Janie has apparently become an autonomous person, whose first independent choice is to replace her double-consciousness concerning Logan with whatever might result from marriage with Joe. Because of the domineering nature of Joe's big voice, however, he "did not represent sun-up and pollen and blooming trees" (29). Thus, "Her old thoughts were going to come in handy now, but new words would have to be made and said to fit them" (32). The new words would express Janie's externalistic sense of self as Joe's wife while her old thoughts would remain focused on love, sex, and personal answers in life's struggles. Rather than simply replacing this old sense of self with one more responsive to her new role, as recommended by Nanny that is,[7] Janie now intends to embody herself in speech-acts enhancing both the old sense and the new one.

Because she has underestimated Joe's declaring his intention to become "a big voice," however, Janie underestimates the difficulty of performing the kind of speech-acts she seeks with him. On the one hand, Joe's big voice "keeps us in some way we ain't natural wid one 'nother" (46).[8] On the other hand, his big voice constrains Janie's public appearances,[9] and scorns the mistakes she makes in his store.[10] The type of double-consciousness created by such authoritarianism is first explicitly identified when Joe suppresses Janie's speaking at a public celebration during their initial year in Eatonville. "Janie made her face laugh after a short pause, but it wasn't too easy" (43).

Apparently, Janie knows at age eighteen, seventeen years earlier than indicated by Gates above, that she sometimes has a type of double-consciousness. Her externalistic sense of self as Joe's wife, for example, sometimes prevents her from performing self-embodying speech-acts she assumes would feel satisfying. It does so by preventing her from seeking personal answers as a public speaker in the community's life.

In other situations, however, the speech-acts involved by Janie's sense of self as Joe's wife do seem satisfying. Externalistic success, that is, allows internalistic success. For example, Janie seems quite satisfied in expressing appreciation for Joe's eliminating a certain form of mule-baiting in Eatonville. "Jody, dat wuz uh mighty fine thing fuh you tuh do. 'Tain't everybody would have thought of it, 'cause it ain't no everyday thought. Freein' dat mule makes uh mighty big man outa you" (58). To this extent, Janie seems to avoid double-consciousness. Indeed, even when Janie is self-abnegating, she does not seem self-pitying or self-contemptuous. Rather, she knowingly, willingly, and self-respectfully adopts the best available alternative from her point of view. "'But Ah hates disagreement and confusion, so Ah better not talk. It makes it hard tuh git along'" (57). Stokely Carmichael observes that many self-respecting civil rights leaders have employed related strategies of self-abnegation.

> [W]hat Dr. King meant by discipline and control . . . was . . . actually taking control of a situation and an opponent, actually imposing your will even as the rains blows down on your unresisting head. . . . You merely had to eliminate everything in your behavior—word, deed, look, gesture, or body language—that might provoke or nourish the impulse to violence, the evolutionary conditioning to battle, in your opponent. . . . The broad general terms of his [Bayard Rustin's] responses were standard nonviolent techniques, carefully controlled and developed for effect much like in a theatrical performance. (Carmichael/Thelwell, 2003: 169, 171)

As Joe continues suppressing and scorning Janie's acts, however, "The spirit of the marriage left the bedroom and took to living in the parlor" (71). Indeed, after Joe slaps her for a burnt dinner in their seventh year of marriage, Janie's sense of self as his wife almost never seems reconciled with any of her senses of self as struggling for personal answers in life. Rather, as observed above, she now knows how to prevent her inside from mixing with her outside. As a result, the acts she performs as Joe's wife are almost never satisfying in ways she most seeks. Janie thus seems to have one of the types of double-consciousness identified by Du Bois, the type in which two senses of self are in a "warring" relationship.[11] But this conflict between externalistic and internalistic success is complicated by the fact that, for a long time, none of Janie's speech-acts seem to embody a sense of self-pity or self-contempt. Indeed, some clearly embody a sense of self-respect, as illustrated in Janie's response to general insults about women delivered by Joe and by several store-talkers.[12]

> Sometimes God gits familiar wid us womenfolks too and talks His inside business. He told me how surprised He was 'bout y'all turning out so smart after Him makin' yuh different; and how surprised y'all is goin' tuh be if you ever find out you don't know half as much 'bout us as you think you do. (75)

Here, many philosophers would observe that Janie seems embodied in speech with the illocutionary attitude of declaring the basic equality of women generally and herself specifically. As considered in chapter 3, Strawson is one of the few philosophers who also observe that a person in Janie's position can therefore develop a relatively satisfying sense of self. With the caveat observed there, Strawson considers that a person who bequeaths a gift might, as a result, "take some satisfaction in the thought" of having issued the bequest. Here, Janie might take some satisfaction in the thought of having issued her declaration of equality. In particular, she might be aware of herself as then embodied in a self-respecting declaration. She cannot feel love or sexual happiness with Joe, or the playfulness of being "natural," the satisfying senses she prefers. However, Janie does seem to create or to extend a sense of self-respect while struggling with Joe.[13] Her speech, that is, seems to enhance a satisfying sense of self. It seems internalistically delivered with affective energy.

Janie's Access to Internalistic Affective Energy with Joe
We saw in chapter 3 that Austin recognizes that our speech can influence our feelings. "Saying something will often, or even normally, produce certain consequential effects upon the feelings . . . of the speaker." As observed in our Introduction, Dylan's singing is sometimes presented in this way. "It's a statement that maybe you can say to make yourself feel better. It's as if you were talking to yourself." Wilder (2002) suggests a related point about one's race-based sense of self.

> Langston Hughes [1926: 694] summarized this emancipated racial sensibility in a formulation that the Negritude writers later enjoyed quoting: "We younger Negro artists who create now intend to express our individual dark-skinned selves without fear or shame. If white people are pleased, we are glad. If they are not, it doesn't matter." (175–76)

As discussed in chapter 2, on the other hand, Hurston warns against our using this force in frivolous ways. "Course, talkin' don't amount tuh uh hill uh beans when yuh can't do nothin' else."

For long after they are married, however, none of Janie's speech-acts with Joe seem frivolous. Instead, the senses of self apparently embodied in the illocutionary forces of her utterances remain calmly, determinedly, and justifiably self-respecting. Nonetheless, her coping with Joe's responses to such speech eventually convinces Janie her soul has lost its fight. "The years took all the fight out of Janie's face. For a while she thought it was gone from her soul" (76).[14] She is now at least vulnerable to double-consciousness in the self-pitying sense emphasized by Du Bois. In response, Janie decides to "lie" about Joe's significance for her and, as considered in chapter 2 above, shortly gains the urine-and-perfume-revelation as well as the wind-blown-hair-revelation.[15] More generally, she feels "reconciled to things" (77).

Occasionally, furthermore, Janie still seems embodied in the illocutionary force of a self-respecting speech-act, as illustrated in her finally responding to an insult by Joe with one of her own.[16]

> Ah reckon Ah looks mah age too. But Ah'm uh woman every inch of me, and Ah know it. Dat's uh whole lot more'n *you* kin say. You big-bellies round here and put out a lot of brag, but 'tain't nothin' to it but yo' big voice. Humph! Talkin' 'bout *me* lookin' old! When you pull down yo' britches, you look lak de change uh life. (79)

Here, Janie seems to intend that Joe recognize she has an insultingly declarative attitude toward him. As Nagel maintains more generally in chapter 4, Janie wants Joe to "feel" that she declares her insult. We observed in chapter 2 that Strasberg agrees. He thinks our most important speech is "a means of sharing one's individual way of experiencing"—in this case, a means of Janie's sharing her insulting declaration so that Joe recognizes it. Presumably, Janie does this intentionalistically. Because she is already aware of her insulting declaration regarding Joe, she presents the utterance so that its performative success depends on its statemental success. To grasp Janie's utterance as she intends it, Joe must recognize what is already true for her.

In response, Joe "struck Janie with all his might" (80), and later tends to shun her. Thus, Janie eventually tells Pheoby she feels "'stone dead from standin' still and tryin' tuh smile'" (83). This need not involve double-consciousness in the sense of self-pity or self-contempt. It would nonetheless be pernicious. By virtue of her role as Joe's wife, that is, Janie now feels "dead." She does not feel aware of herself at all within this role. Like representational actors, she apparently uses acts of communication, smiles in particular, which typically achieve certain perlocutionary results with Joe. On the one hand, however, such perlocutionary results are not forthcoming in the manner with which Janie is familiar. There are thus no relevant perlocutionary results for which she feels responsible. On the other hand, Janie does not take advantage of the opportunity to focus on the illocutionary attitudes appropriate to her speech-acts, to act presentationally or with affective energy. Thus, she has no sense of self as embodied in those speech-acts. The process continues until Joe lies dying of kidney illness.

Janie's speech as Joe dies, however, clearly embodies a sense of her, one that is self-respecting rather than self-pitying or self-contemptuous. "Naw, you gointuh listen tuh me one time befo' you die" (86). As previously observed, the illocutionary attitude apparently embodied in this speech-act is a self-respecting demand that Joe listen to Janie's declaring surprise, given their courtship, at the way he has superimposed a sense of her as inadequate onto her own sense of self-respect. Though Janie does not seem happy about the current exchange, the sense of self embodied in her contribution does seem reasonably satisfying. Her internalistic sense of self as answering life's problems in a satisfying way is thus not always suppressed by her externalistic role as Joe's wife. The latter does not always involve any sense of double-consciousness considered by Du Bois. Janie's role as Joe's wife does not always prevent access to internalistic affective energy, to speech-acts that enhance a satisfying sense of self.

Summary of Changes in Janie's Speech-Acts and Senses of Self with Joe

In sum, discussion of illocutionary speech-acts can help to explicate the development of Janie's senses of self with Joe. Most importantly, it specifies that every meaningful utterance can be regarded as embodying an illocutionary attitude as a speaker's sense of self. Speakers with internalistic affective energy can take advantage of this by embodying in their speech-acts illocutionary attitudes that are satisfying.

Janie can be interpreted as repeatedly using this opportunity to offset occasional conflicts between her externalistic sense of self as Joe's wife and her internalistic sense of self as struggling for personal answers in life. She "reconciles" these two by typically identifying herself with the illocutionary attitudes of role-appropriate utterances involving a sense of self-respect. For a while, this involves her speaking "lies" about Joe's value for her. After the second of Joe's slaps, however, Janie focuses only on the perlocutionary forces of her utterances. She therefore loses the ability to speak with internalistic affective energy, as satisfyingly embodied in her speech-acts. This continues until she confronts Joe while he lies dying. By then embodying a demand of attention, however, Janie's speech-act fulfills her sense of self as struggling for personal answers in life, and hence feels satisfying. There is no feeling of double-consciousness involved by the relationship between her internalistic and externalistic senses of self.

We see this by considering the illocutionary/perlocutionary distinction as combined with the concept of affective energy and with the internalistic/externalistic distinction. The latter two are therefore more fully explicated than otherwise. Correlatively, our use of the illocutionary/perlocutionary distinction is broadened.

6. Representationalism as a Source of Internalistically Successful Affective Energy

After Joe's death, Janie "starched and ironed her face, forming it into just what people wanted to see" (88). This, however, is the last of her acts that

Janie might construe as a lie. It is the last act she performs to fulfill some externalistic role that she might regard as opposed to her sense of self as struggling for satisfying answers concerning life. As expressed in free indirect discourse, Janie was thereafter "just basking in freedom" (93). "She would have the rest of her life to do as she pleased" (89).[17]

Janie reflects that her pear-tree-revelation had exposed "a jewel down inside herself and she had wanted to walk where people could see her and gleam it around" (90). The externalistic constraints of marriage with Logan and with Joe had prevented this, however. Thus, Janie "was saving up feelings for some man she had never seen" (72), and she remains aware of "lonesomeness" until Tea Cake appears. "Once upon uh time, Ah never 'spected nothin', Tea Cake, but bein' dead from the standin' still and tryin' tuh laugh. But you come 'long and made somethin' outa me. So Ah'm thankful fuh anything we come through together" (167).

By virtue of this and other passages, many critics agree with Wall (1997b: 713) that Tea Cake "has been a cultural mentor and spiritual guide" for Janie. Washington (1998), for example, thinks Janie's interior life reveals more about Tea Cake than about Janie.

> Hurston has not given us an unambiguously heroic female character. She puts Janie on the track of autonomy, self-realization, and independence, but she also places Janie in the position of romantic heroine as the object of Tea Cake's quest, at times so subordinate to the magnificent presence of Tea Cake that even her interior life reveals more about him than about her. (xv)[18]

An observation by Lane (1997) helps to explain some of how this might occur. Specifically, it suggests how one's affective energy can be internalistically successful as based initially on representationalism.

Lane's observation is related to that of Michael Caine considered in chapter 4—namely, we can enhance our communicative success by appropriating certain manners of speech displayed by someone else. What Lane adds to Caine is that we can also improve our speech-embodied senses of self in this way. While Lane advances the observation concerning film stars, it clearly holds also concerning role models with whom we exchange speech in daily life, as was true of Janie with Tea Cake.

> Men like [Robert] Mitchum and [Jimmy] Stewart suggest not just what cinema is all about but what, in a more difficult sense, it is for. We face up to them, and they, in turn, show us a few more angles at which we can—if we choose—face the prospect of our own lives. . . . [T]he Hollywood tour guides who practice

their Jimmy Stewart impressions, like the Woody Allen who pulled his lips tight against his teeth in "Play It Again, Sam," are not simply indulging a whim or a knack; they want to stretch their imaginations and work out how much cooler or more approachable the world must be to Stewart or Bogart. (32)

Regarding Janie in particular, her desire to "laugh and play" is finally satisfied by learning to imitate Tea Cake's angular form of speech-acts: abrupt, incomplete, or unexpected.

> "Evenin', Mis' Starks. Could yuh lemme have uh pound uh knuckle puddin' till Saturday? Ah'm sho tuh pay yuh then."
> "You needs ten pounds, Mr. Tea Cake. Ah'll let yuh have all Ah got and you needn't bother 'bout payin' it back." (98)

Thus, although she had never before used an angular form of speech with anyone except Tea Cake, Janie employs it when she returns to Eatonville after his rabies-infected death and Pheoby welcomes her with food. "Here, Pheoby, tak yo' ole plate. Ah ain't got a bit of use for a empty dish. Dat grub sho come in handy" (5).

As observed of Charlie's playful speech in chapter 3 above, much of Janie's speech here seems delivered conventionalistically. The existence of a playful demand that Pheoby take back her plate, in particular, depends on Pheoby's agreeing that the utterance is a playful demand. (One version of tone and rhythm appropriate for this interpretation is presented in Halle Berry's portrayal of Janie in the film version of *Their Eyes Were Watching God* [Martin, 2005].) The truth that Janie's illocutionary attitude is a playful demand is a shared truth if it exists at all. On the other hand, Janie's expression of appreciation seems delivered intentionalistically. She regards as true that her illocutionary attitude is appreciating, and invites Pheoby to recognize this by recognizing Janie regards it as true independently of Pheoby's agreement.

We noted in chapter 1 that Gates observes this use of satisfying speech helps to define Janie's search for self. "For Hurston, the search for a telling form of language . . . defines the search for the self. . . . On the broadest level, *Their Eyes* depicts the search for identity and self-understanding of an Afro-American woman." For performists, in short, the illocutionary attitudes embodied in speech-acts can literally be a speaker's senses of self. This, even if those speech-acts are originally learned representationally, as imitating those of respected role models.

Representationalism as a Source of Internalistically Successful Affective Energy for Some Speakers

Bob Dylan, a master of an American oral tradition, sometimes objects to learning a form of speech-acts representationally, as imitating the form of one or more other people. (As observed in note 13 of chapter 4, Ramblin' Jack Elliot maintains that Dylan did use imitation to learn some of Elliott's songs.)

> What made the real blues singers so great is that they were able to state all the problems they had; but at the same time, they were standing outside of them and could look at them. And in that way, they had them beat. What's depressing today is that many young singers are trying to get *inside* the blues, forgetting that those older singers used them to get *outside* their troubles. (as quoted by Hentoff, 1963)

Judy Collins, on the other hand, thinks the representational way of learning a form of speech-acts can be satisfying.[19]

> You [Dylan] gave words to a world where we all had something to lean on, however fragile. We knew the slender thread of "what is," a thread we had constructed out of God knows what grit and dreams and smoke. . . . I have a fantasy that back in Minnesota you had a high tenor voice as a child. Right behind the raspiness in your singing there is a sweetness that never got lost, the tone always true to our hearts and memories. As I sang these songs [written by Dylan] I looked for you. I found you. And I found me. (1993)

In contrast, Odetta appropriated Dylan's songs without doing so representationally.

> Because of the strength of Bob Dylan's songs, especially in his presentation of them, it is sometimes quite difficult to resist imitating him. But something did not allow me to become a reflection. I believe it is known as the "ego." Thus, when Mr. Dylan's songs and I got to working together, I made some lovely discoveries; one being Dylan's own turn with the melody, whether his own or adapted. Another discovery—the young "old" man; i.e., the wonder of how young Dylan can reduce to words such powerfully emotional content which comes out of wisdom usually attributed to a long span in time and living experience. (1965)

As we have noted, many critics think Janie responds to Tea Cake more in the manner of Collins than in that of Odetta. Even if so, it seems possible not only to develop a satisfying sense of self within this representational approach to speech-acts but also to be regarded as genuinely creative.

> When we see Jack [Ramblin' Jack Elliott] on the stage now he is Jack and no longer an imitation of Woody [Guthrie]. He's proven that it's possible to learn an idiom and a style one was not born to, but came to love later in life, and he's proven also that you can emerge from this period of imitation into being genuinely creative on your own; something that needs proving in this modern world when there's so much confusion among young people as to the value of imitating between the value of just being yourself.[20] (Pete Seeger, as quoted by Yaryan, 1965)

Indeed, Aristotle might be interpreted as supporting the representational approach to internalistic success.

> The same is true of appetites and feelings of anger; some men become temperate and good-tempered, others self-indulgent and irascible, by behaving in one way or the other in the appropriate circumstances. This is why the activities we exhibit must be of a certain kind; it is because the states of character correspond to the differences between these. It makes no small difference, then, whether we form habits of one kind or of another from our very youth; it makes a very great difference, or rather all the difference. (1103b: 17–26)

Of course, Aristotle is most concerned with such features of character as courage and prudence whereas Dylan, Collins, and Odetta might be interpreted as also, or instead, concerned with such features of style as rhythm and tone of speech. Regardless, Collins describes success with a representational approach to acts of communication in which we learn to appreciate a sense of self available for speech-embodiment by focusing primarily on imitating tones and rhythms we have observed to be perlocutionarily successful regarding certain speech-acts by another person. What the observation by Collins, and by Lane, emphasizes is that one can eventually learn to achieve communicative success while focused on these tones and rhythms. Once this is learned, furthermore, Collins and Lane observe we can be satisfied with whatever senses of self seems embodied in such speech-acts.

Dylan finds this possibility depressing, apparently because he thinks "great" speech-acts must express a previously existing sense of self, presentationalism. That is, he interprets "the real blues singers" as using sung speech-acts to embody certain previously existing senses of self. But, on the one hand, speech-acts can be used to enhance some sense of self for a speaker as well as to evoke some perlocutionary result in other people. On the other hand, we can learn to identify ourselves via the illocutionary attitudes embodied in our speech-acts even if we initially learn these speech-acts representationally, even if we initially learn them simply by imitating a mentor's tone and rhythm. Knobler

(1989) explains the point with specific reference to those who began to sing folk music during the sixties. "Folk music, for all the easy cynicism about 'Rights' to empathy, or 'legitimate' emotions, can finally form a foundation, grant you a background you may not possess but certainly can feel."

Hurston remains right, of course, that "talkin' don't amount tuh uh hill uh beans when yuh can't do nothin' else." The point is that performists can learn to enact a role with internalistic affective energy even if they begin to learn that role while enacting it representationally as imitating the acting styles of other people.

Summary of Changes in Janie's Speech-Acts and Speech-Embodied Senses of Self

In sum, Hurston presents Janie as maintaining a sense of self-respect more or less continuously while evolving from Logan's wife to Eatonville matriarch. The illocutionary/perlocutionary distinction helps to explicate Hurston's technique. Hurston presents Janie's implicit illocutionary speech-acts, her demanding and teasing ones for example, so we recognize her speech-embodied self-respect amidst adverse as well as auspicious circumstances. Some of these emphasize intentionalism while others emphasize conventionalism. Some emphasize externalism while others emphasize internalism, or both externalism and internalism. Some emphasize representationalism rather than presentationalism or affective energy—they emphasize perlocutionary force rather than illocutionary force. We therefore understand the externalism/internalism and representational/presentational distinctions better by understanding how each involves, or fails to involve, an illocutionarily intended act of communication. We understand illocutionary acts better by understanding they are parts of social performances delivered within a web of communicative forces which is not limited to those usually associated with conventionalism and intentionalism. Chapter 6 will develop this point with respect to the Nigerian political prisoners facing immediate execution considered in our Introduction.

Notes

1. Eatonville, specifically, which Hurston (1942/1996: 1) claims was the first all-Black town to be incorporated in the United States. This claim is more or less corroborated by a Library of Congress official.

> According to Romeo B. Garrett in *Famous First Facts about Negroes* (Arno Press, 1972), Eatonville, Florida became the first town in the United States to be chartered specifically

for Black people when it received its charter of incorporation in 1883. . . . [T]he date for the incorporation of Eatonville is corroborated in the Booker T. Washington papers. . . . [W]hat with the vagaries of research and the human condition, any designation of "first" is seldom either settling or settled. (Fletcher, 1976)

The unsettled nature of this issue is demonstrated by a photocopy of Eatonville's Notice of Incorporation held by the Maitland, Florida Public Library, which presents 1887 as the date of Eatonville's incorporation—cf. Johnson (1887: 1). Thus, Salamone (1988) observes that "Freed slaves incorporated Princeville, North Carolina, in 1885, two years before Eatonville became a Florida town, according to records in the Florida and North Carolina state departments." The period that concerns us, in any case, brackets our last century's beginning.

2. Gates (1988: 209, which contains the bracketed comment), who quotes Ducrot and Todorov (1979: 303). Gates's discussion of free indirect discourse also draws from those of Ginsberg (1977), Hough (1970), McHale (1978), Pascal (1977), and Ullmann (1957).

3. Of relevance to the discussion below, Janie's pear-tree-revelation has a component that need not be associated with either love or sex, a "struggle with life" in which she must seek a "personal answer" (Hurston, 1937/1998: 11).

4. Gates uses "the word *double* here intentionally to echo W. E. B. Du Bois's metaphor for the Afro-American's peculiar psychology of citizenship" (207).

It is a peculiar sensation, this double-consciousness, this sense of always looking at one's self through the eyes of others, of measuring one's soul by the tape of a world that looks on in amused contempt and pity. One ever feels his twoness—an American, a Negro; two souls, two thoughts, two unreconciled strivings; two warring ideals in one dark body, whose dogged strength alone keeps it from being torn asunder. (Du Bois, 1903/1989: 3)

5. Gates thus thinks Janie does not come to consciousness until she is thirty-five years old. Janie, on the other hand, thinks her conscious life began to evolve at age sixteen. "She thought awhile and decided that her conscious life had commenced at Nanny's gate" (Hurston, 1937/1998: 10) after her sexual awakening under the blooming pear tree. In sections 4 and 5, we consider some of the changes in Janie's evolving self-consciousness beginning with her childhood.

6. For women, but not for men, Hurston thinks "The dream is the truth. Then they act and do things accordingly" (1937/1998: 1). Wall (1997b) therefore argues that "by denying Janie the right to follow her dreams, Nanny inhibits her quest for [internalistic] self-hood" (526).

7. "'Heah you got uh prop [Logan] tuh lean on all yo' bawn days, and big protection" and yet "you come worryin' me 'bout love'" (23).

8. Hurston does not explicitly explain why some but not all acts are natural. Later, however, she apparently does so implicitly by contrasting Joe with people who "'want tuh laugh and play'" while he "made an attack upon her position" (62). Hemenway (1997/1980: 44) quotes from his interview with Arna Bontemps (18

November 1970; New Haven, Conn.) that Hurston often used "natural" to describe the dialect of uneducated Southern farmers, workers, preachers, and merchants, the people who had raised her in Eatonville—at (1935/1990: 249) and at (1942/1996: 283), for example.

9. Because Joe prizes Janie's status as the mayor's wife, he commands "*You* ain't goin' off in all dat mess uh commonness" (60).

10. "'She sho don't talk much. De way he rears and pitches in de store sometimes when she make uh mistake is sort of ungodly, but she don't seem to mind at all'" (50).

11. Hurston (1942/1996) describes her own "insides" as sometimes warring with her own circumstances.

> Sometimes I didn't suit the people [in her first jobs after leaving home]. Sometimes the people didn't suit me. Sometimes my insides tortured me so that I was restless and unstable.... I was doing none of the things I wanted to do. I had to do numerous uninteresting things I did not want to do, and it was tearing me to pieces. (97)

12. "'Somebody got to think for women and chillun and chickens and cows. I god, they sho don't think none theirselves'" (71).

13. Of course, a speech-act sometimes creates a new sense of self for a speaker, as when one recognizes her love for a partner only after first uttering "I've fallen in love with you," or some such. Let us not consider whether there is any typical priority between speech-acts and senses of self. Even if Janie's declaring her equality here results from her already feeling self-respect, her declaring it "dramatically" can, as observed by Mamet and by Hagen in chapter 2, surely expand this previously existing sense of self.

14. As discussed in chapter 2, Hemenway and Plant explicate Hurston's concept of soul as being a person's ability to use speech, and other acts of communication, in transforming her senses of self so they are satisfying. Within this interpretation, Hurston thinks a person loses that ability when her soul loses its fight. We address this concept of soul again in chapter 6.

15. Hurston provides no further examples of Janie's lies. Perhaps they would be presented over-the-top somewhat as we suggested in chapter 3 might be true of John with Ole Massa, or of J.T. with Missa Charlie.

16. "'I god amighty! A woman stay round uh store till she get old as Methusalem and still can't cut a little thing like a plug of tobacco! Don't stand dere rollin' yo' pop eyes at me wid yo' rump hangin' nearly to yo' knees!'" (78).

It is perhaps worth observing that Janie is quite attractive physically. When she returns to Eatonville four years later, for example, "The men noticed her firm buttocks like she had grapefruits in her hip pockets" as well as "her pugnacious breasts trying to bore holes in her shirt" (2).

17. "The young girl was gone, but a handsome woman had taken her place" (87). Janie is not just a woman, in other words, not just one who has recovered independent responsibility for her senses of self. Rather, Janie is a woman who has become

handsome. She has done so by coping in her typically self-respecting way with the various struggles considered above. Of course, this leaves unanswered whether Janie's handsomeness could have endured her ongoing suppression had Joe not died when he did.

18. Janie appreciates Tea Cake's magnificent features despite several disturbing ones. He purloins and gambles away her money, eventually returned. He accepts sexual advances from another woman. Except for his strength and courage, Janie would have drowned by acquiescing to Tea Cake's poor judgment about a coming hurricane.

19. Without specifying previous troubles, Cary Grant famously described himself as using speech and other acts to get outside a previously existing sense of self. "I pretended to be somebody I wanted to be and finally, I became that person. Or he became me" (as quoted by Browne and Browne [2001: 340]).

20. According to Elliott himself, one can imitate while creating one's own sources. "I have always created my own sources, but I still sing Woody's songs. While a lot of people don't think I'm imitating Woody, I still feel I am in a way, you know, like he's looking over my shoulder" (1974: 6).

CHAPTER SIX

Performism in the World

1. Predecessors

Writers often describe their concentration on speech-acts as satisfying. According to Nikos Kazantzakis, for example, "I never relived his Life and Passion with such intensity, such understanding and love, as during the days and nights when I wrote *The Last Temptation of Christ*" (1955/1988: 2). Paul Simon provides a related example that involves spoken as well as written speech-acts.

> PLAYBOY: What did you expect creatively from a Simon and Garfunkel tour [in Europe after the free, 1981, reunion concert in Central Park]?
>
> SIMON: Nothing. I thought I was going to get an emotional experience from it. I felt I wasn't really present for Simon and Garfunkel the first time around.
>
> PLAYBOY: Where were you?
>
> SIMON: I wasn't home, the same way that I wasn't present for the concert in the park when it was happening. I mean, a phenomenon occurs and it's recognized as a phenomenon. But because you're in the middle of it, you just think that it's your life—until it's over. And then you look back and say, "What an *unusual* thing happened to me in the Sixties." So there it was. A chance to go and re-experience, to a certain degree, what I hadn't really experienced the first time. Some of those hits from the Sixties I just had no interest in anymore, musically. But I had an interest in experiencing what it was like being the person who wrote and sang those songs. (Simon, 1984: 51)

Many of Hurston's commentators believe this type of satisfaction true of her own writing, and a source of her own "inner growth." "Giving spiritual substance to her characters through the subtle variations of language within their voices . . . was in a very real sense giving substance and form to her own 'self'" (Holloway, 1987: 115).

Kane (1995) presents a related interpretation of Anselm's ontological proof of God's existence. According to Kane, Anselm's proof emphasizes that anyone's being appropriately focused on a certain idea, whether written or spoken or otherwise contemplated, can yield an understanding which is satisfying.

> Anselm put his proof in the context of a prayer or meditation. In effect, he said, "Oh (unknown) God whom I seek, help me to get the idea of You right so I will understand that You exist." . . . God is different. Meditate on that fact, Anselm tells us. . . . [I]f you understand what God is really like, a being than whom none greater can be thought, you'll get it: God exists. (1995: 158–59)

Interestingly, this view of Christianity confronts the type of challenge John Mbiti (1969/1990/1996) directs against Senghor's view of negritude.

> Negritude is, then, a comfortable exercise for the elite who wants, seeks and finds it when he looks at the African Zamani [roughly, the period between day before yesterday and the "unlimited past"] and hopes for an African future. . . . You only need to imagine it and you will be able to identify it; be lucid about it and you will be able to see it. Negritude is because it is said to be. (76)

Advocates of theism as well as those of negritude might, of course, reject this type of criticism as missing the point that each way of concentrating our attention can be what Kane calls "a salutary undertaking." Specifically, each can enhance an awareness that is satisfying, which sometimes seems more important than whether any associated belief can be empirically justified.[1]

Mbiti's criticism also overlooks the distinction between that which is explicitly addressed within and that which is implicitly part of many Africana events. Mbiti is right that negritude "has neither dogmas nor taboos, neither feast days nor ceremonies" (76). Whether or not anyone "in the villages . . . subscribes to its philosophical expressions" (76), however, many villagers might well employ the forms of speech Senghor celebrates. Hurston thinks the citizens of Eatonville do so.

Of course, what we know of these people results from Hurston's ethnography and fiction rather than from scientific consensus. As is sometimes true of academic philosophy, then, Hurston's fiction and ethnography suggest new avenues for scientific research without proving that any one of them has already been productive.² To whatever extent Hurston's fictional characters are representative of performists generally, however, the evolving relationships between their speech-acts and what seem to be their senses of self are informative. To that extent, in particular, they suggest one explanation for why and how the Nigerian prisoners considered in our Introduction sang as they awaited imminently inevitable execution. "[W]e can rely on the story to tell us not only what might have happened, but also what is happening at an unspecified time and place" (Minh-Ha, 1987: 4).

2. Speech-Acts before Imminently Inevitable Death

The last speech of condemned prisoners is sometimes intended to inspire supporters. Joe Hill's "Don't waste any time mourning. Organize!" is one of the most prominent American examples. The last speech of the condemned political prisoners in Nigeria was not viewed in this way, however, by many of my friends who commented. Instead, most viewed a prisoner's singing as self-inspiring, as a use of speech to influence his sense of self. That is, they viewed it internalistically, as intended to enhance the most satisfying sense of self available within a prisoner's trying circumstance.

The singing was thus understood as Nathan Hale's reputed regret, expressed to his executioners, might be understood. Indeed, I was told that the prisoners' songs typically declared their patriotism. Some observers thought such a man, like presentational actors, already had a felt-sense of courage, which his singing enhanced. Others thought such a man, like Mamet's outward-directed actors, acquired a felt-sense of courage, if at all, only after his singing began. Performism helps explain why and how the prisoners might sing as they did, at least regarding the former case.

One's Sense of Self as Embodied in One's Speech-Acts

The performist explanation agrees with those involved in the professional theater in three ways. First, enactments can be performed off-stage as well as on-. "Just finding ourselves where we are carries with it the invitation to make that 'here' a stage. . . . Our skin and the nervous tension in our muscles quicken as we realize that though our environment may close in on us, it is also open to enactment" (Holt, 1992: 78). Second, utterances regarded as enactments can embody senses of self. "Manners, habit, style, good and bad behavior, matter because they are how we take our place" (Holt, 1992: 79). Third, techniques from professional acting can be useful in this regard off-stage as well as on-.

> [W]e all have behavior that defines the character we have created for ourselves as we've grown up from infancy into our adult lives. . . . Anyone who wishes to live freely and honestly should take up the challenge to discover and examine [certain techniques from Batson's approach to professional acting]. . . . Through this process of discovery, you may even find new ways of building your own character and of identifying and maintaining your own moral center. (Batson, 2007: 7, 28)

The performist explanation also agrees with Hurston that certain people typically take advantage of the opportunity for enacting various senses of self offstage, though performism does not limit the scope of such people by race as she does. "Hurston created performative language to emphasize that ritualized behavior is preeminent in the black cultures she studied, which led her to conclude that drama is the ultimate quality of life among blacks 'the world over'" (Hill, 1996: xx–xxi).

The Nigerian prisoners who sang typically took their places in soccer stadiums filled with thousands of hostile fellow-citizens as well as with guards and machine-gunners. If performists, the prisoners could have appreciated two of Hurston's insights in particular. First, "You can't beat nobody down so low till you can rob 'em of they will" (1937/1998: 16). Second, as observed in chapter 1, "No matter how joyful or how sad the case there is sufficient poise for drama. Everything is acted out. . . . [I]t satisfies the soul of its creator." If performists, the prisoners would have sung with internalistic affective energy to focus on some satisfying sense of self available within the confines of their situation. This internalistic sense of self would have been the illocutionary attitude embodied in the declarations of patriotism within their sung speech-acts.

Unlike the executions of the Nigerian political prisoners, the execution of Saddam Hussein is widely available to Westerners via internet videos. In addition to the official video provided by the Iraqi government, an apparently unofficial video was published.[3] The latter includes audio of Hussein's dialogue with the crowd of witnesses. CNN (2006) provides a transcript of a translation of this dialogue. Carol Lin, the CNN anchor addressing that dialogue, describes the speech of witnesses as "taunts" and that of a "defiant" Hussein as "repeating their taunts sarcastically."

SADDAM HUSSEIN, FMR. IRAQI PRESIDENT (through translator): Prayers be upon the Prophet Mohammad and on his family. And glorify the mighty and curse his enemy.

UNIDENTIFIED GROUP: Muqtada, Muqtada, Muqtada . . .

HUSSEIN: Muqtada. Is this how you show your bravery as men?

UNIDENTIFIED MALE: Straight to hell.

HUSSEIN: Is this the bravery of Arabs?

UNIDENTIFIED MALE: Long live Mohammad Baqir Sadr.

UNIDENTIFIED MALE: Straight to hell.

UNIDENTIFIED MALE: Please, I am begging you not to. The man is being executed.

HUSSEIN: I bear witness that there is no god but God and that Mohammad is the messenger of God. And I bear witness that there is no god but God. . . .

Like Lin, we have direct access to Hussein's speech-acts, not to his senses of self. So, we cannot be sure that Hussein would have identified his senses of self as defiant or as sarcastic. On the other hand, his face- and body-language as well as his tone and rhythm of voice between the prayers seem well-suited to embody such senses. For that matter, the tone and rhythm of voice during each of the two prayers seem well-suited to embody a devotional sense of self. Such states of mind are among those likely to be most satisfying when one confronts imminently inevitable death in a situation such as Hussein's. They can be enhanced by embodiment as the illocutionary attitudes associated with one's speech-acts—declarations of devotion, of defiance and sarcasm, and of devotion again for example.

Viewing One's Speech-Acts Intentionalistically
If Hussein were a performist at his execution, he could more easily interpret the illocutionary attitudes embodied in his speech-acts intentionalistically than conventionalistically. The reason here is the same as that regarding Tea Cake's response to Janie's skepticism about his picnic-invitation, as considered in chapter 4 above. Specifically, only within an intentionalistic interpretation does the statement associated with an illocutionary speech-act seem true to a speaker regardless of whether the speech-act is communicatively successful. Only for a thus-focused Hussein would the sense of self as declaring defiance and sarcasm that seems illocutionarily embodied in his speech-acts be relatively independent of how anyone else responds. Most likely, Hussein intended to communicate this declaration effectively so that the witnesses would recognize it for what it was. Regardless of whether the witnesses even heard him, however, Hussein could continue with reflexively related declarations of defiance and sarcasm relatively easily so long as he presented them intentionalistically. In this sense, it would be somewhat

irrelevant that the correlative facts be created, declarations of defiance and sarcasm.

Similarly, if the Nigerian political prisoners were performists, they could more easily interpret the illocutionary attitude embodied in their speech-acts intentionalistically than conventionalistically. Only for a thus-focused prisoner would the sense of self as declaring patriotism, which seems illocutionarily embodied in his speech-acts, be relatively independent of how anyone else responds. He could therefore continue with reflexively related singing relatively easily when surrounded by hostile listeners who might not recognize his speech-acts as being declarations of patriotism. For example, they might instead interpret those speech-acts as extravagant excuses and, by jeering, negatively superimpose that interpretation on the prisoner's own speech-embodied sense of self.[4]

Viewing One's Speech-Acts Conventionalistically
As might be expected, some of the Nigerian political prisoners who began their last walks with singing could not sustain their songs. One obvious reason is that suggested by Omoregbe in our Introduction, that fear of losing all which is of value simply overwhelms one's concern with pluck. Another is suggested by the discussion immediately above. If a prisoner began his last walk while singing as a performist with a conventionalistic interpretation of the illocutionary attitude embodied in his speech-acts, then the statemental success of those speech-acts as declarations of patriotism would depend on their performative success. The truth of the statement associated with those speech-acts would depend, that is, on listeners' showing they understood those speech-acts as intended to satisfy a convention whose satisfaction creates a declaration of patriotism. Since most listeners were hostile, however, they would more likely show prejudice than understanding regarding these speech-acts. Without the relevant understanding, however, no conventionalistic prisoner could regard as true the statements associated with his speech-acts. The sense of self as declaring patriotically which is embodied in those speech-acts would therefore be relatively hard to sustain.

3. Summary and Conclusion

We began our discussion of the speech of condemned prisoners by considering Senghor's view of negritude and Hurston's view of Negro expression. On the one hand, each has helpful observations about how speech is used by some people. On the other hand, Senghor's observations overlap with those of Hurston in several significant ways so that each helps to explicate the other. In developing our discussion, we focused in particular on their observation that the speech of some people involves what Senghor calls their affective energy, their use of speech to enhance their senses of self.

This point was initially explicated with Austin's distinction between the illocutionary and perlocutionary forces of a speech-act. The perlocutionary force of a speech-act produces some change in listeners beyond their understanding the sense and reference of that speech-act—flight after hearing someone utter "The bull is charging," for example. The illocutionary force of a speech-act produces a new fact in the world, beyond listeners' understanding that speech-act's sense and reference, by virtue of which a certain perlocutionary result is reasonable—a warning to produce flight in listeners, for example. A speech-act has illocutionary force in virtue of a speaker's intention to embody a given attitude in that speech-act—warning or declaring, for example. We used the illocutionary attitude that might be embodied in a speech-act to explicate the concept of affective energy. A speaker might enhance her sense of self within some speech-act by attending to her illocutionary attitude at that time.

The intention to embody an illocutionary attitude in a speech-act can be interpreted either conventionalistically or intentionalistically. Conventionalists think the intention is to satisfy a convention whose satisfaction, when recognized by listeners, creates a new fact, which itself makes true the correlative statement that a speaker has the relevant attitude. Intentionalists think the reverse—their (reflexive) intention is that listeners recognize the truth of the statement that a speaker has the relevant attitude which, when recognized, creates the correlative fact.

We used some of the dialogue from Hurston's ethnographic fiction to show that each type of attitude has its use. A conventionalistic attitude is especially appropriate when one is playfully engaging listeners with a sense of self that is relatively tentative—its success rests completely on listeners' recognizing it. A conventionalistic speaker cannot regard the statement associated with an illocutionary speech-act as true unless listeners seem to regard that speech-act as having successfully created a new illocutionary fact. In contrast, an intentionalistic attitude is especially appropriate when one is more seriously engaging listeners with a sense of self that is relatively independent of them. Even if listeners do not understand her illocutionary speech-act, a speaker can regard the statement associated with that speech-act as true. An intentionalistic speaker can therefore continue with reflexively similar speech-acts more easily than can a conventionalistic speaker.

Our discussion of speech-acts continued by observing that theorists of professional acting recommend our employing a distinction between presentational and representational acting offstage as well as on-. This suggestion can be helpfully explicated with the distinction between illocutionary and perlocutionary speech-acts. For a presentationalist such as Hagen, speech-acts involve "the desire to communicate one's own experience and sensations, to make one's self heard and seen." Supposedly, this impacts listeners so as to enhance a speech-act's communicative success. Speaking presentationally can be accomplished by focusing on a sense of self before including it as the illocutionary attitude embodied within one's speech-acts. One makes oneself heard by attending to oneself as warning or declaring, for example, both before and while communicating with warnings or declarations. In contrast, a representationalist attends to types of speech-acts simply as perlocutionarily successful regardless of whether they also communicate her senses of self. To this extent, representationalists can ignore the illocutionary attitudes available for embodiment in their speech-acts.

We then observed that speaking with affective energy is both similar to and different from speaking presentationally. Each type of speaker embodies a sense of self in her speech-acts. But only those with affective energy choose their speech-acts so as to enhance a sense of self. Those who speak with the performist type of affective energy do so by focusing on their illocutionary attitudes. On the other hand, when presentationalists choose and focus on their illocutionary attitudes, they do so to make an impact on their listeners. Obviously, we can focus with affective energy as well as with presentationalism. We can focus on our illocutionary attitudes, that is, to enhance both our senses of self and our communicative success with listeners, though one purpose might be emphasized more than the other. Indeed, as both Mamet and Hagen emphasize, we sometimes become more aware of ourselves as already embodied in our speech-acts while focused primarily on those speech-acts themselves.

Finally, we observed that our performist concept of affective energy is similar to the type of speech identified as internalistic by social psychologists. In each case, speech-acts enhance a sense of self. When they are internalistic, the sense of self is satisfying. When they involve performist affective energy, a speaker's sense of self is embodied as the illocutionary attitude in those speech-acts. Such speech-acts can but need not be also intended externalistically to satisfy the conditions listeners seem to associate with some role in terms of which a speaker seeks to be identified.

In short, the speech-acts of the condemned prisoners we have considered can be interpreted as intended internalistically by intentionalistically embodying declarations of patriotism or of defiance/sarcasm as their illocutionary attitudes. Attending to themselves as thus embodied exposed the prisoners to satisfying senses of self within a stressful circumstance.

Fertilizing Academic Philosophy
In developing this discussion, we have tried to address the lament of Kwame Nkrumah, first president of independent Ghana and two decades previously a doctoral student in philosophy at the London School of Economics.[5] According to Nkrumah, the "academic treatment" employed by philosophers often yields results that are irrelevant to the important issues of life. "It is possible, for instance, to look upon philosophy as a series of abstract systems. When philosophy is so seen, even moral philosophers, with regrettable coyness, say that their preoccupation has nothing to do with life" (1970/1996: 257).

While Nkrumah's lament seems apt for much academic philosophy, we have seen that Sartre, Fingarette, and Nagel directly (as well as Austin, Searle, and Bach and Harnish indirectly) present academic discussions that help in understanding the life-issues addressed by Senghor and by Hurston. In turn, the ways in which Senghor and Hurston address these life-issues expand our understanding of the academic discussions. In Senghor's terms, African values that have been "fertilize[d] and re-invigorate[d]" by the "complementary values of Europe" are thus "offer[ed] for the construction of a civilization which shall embrace all Mankind" (1963: 14).

Notes

1. The ontological argument has been criticized as needlessly elaborate in this regard. Some readers "find in the [ontological] argument an oblique and needlessly elaborate way of eliciting the feeling that there must be some reality that exists by the very necessity of its own nature" ("Theism in Western Thought," 2004). In any case, Kane's modal reformulation of Anselm's argument is flawed, as now shown concerning his ultimate reformulation.

(1') By definition (or necessarily), if God exists, then God necessarily exists.
(2') God's existence is possible (i.e., thinkable, conceivable).
(3") If God's existence is possible, then it is possible that God necessarily exists [from 1'].
(4") It is possible that God necessarily exists [from 2' and 3"].
(5") If something does not in fact exist, then it is not possible that it necessarily exists.
(6') If God does not in fact exist, it is not possible that God necessarily exists [from 5"].

(7) [Thus] God does in fact exist [because the consequent of 6' is denied by 4"]. (1996: 159–60)

Since Kane's premise 2' defines possibility in terms of conceivability, however, 5" must be restatable as

(5''') If something does not in fact exist, then it is not conceivable that it necessarily exists.

But 5''' is plainly false. Many Western children conceive of Santa Claus as existing, for example. Indeed, children with a Liebnizian bent might conceive of Santa Claus as necessarily existing. This could be justified by assuming, first, that ours is the best of all possible worlds and, second, that Santa Claus must be part of such a world. The most obvious way to recast 5''' for truth is

(5'''') If something is conceived as not existing in fact, then it is not conceivable that this thing necessarily exists.

The same, of course, is true of God in particular:

(6") If God is conceived as not existing in fact, then it is not conceivable that God necessarily exists.

Since the consequent of 6" is denied by an appropriate restatement of 4", the antecedent of 6" must be false: it is not the case that God is conceived as not existing in fact. But this result is harmless from the viewpoint of critics who deny the factual existence of something can be derived from thinking about it. Rather, this result shows only how we must think about God, given certain assumptions about Him/Her/Thou, not whether or how God exists in fact. Specifically, our thinking about that Being whose necessary existence is conceived as following from that Being's factual existence prevents our thinking of this Being as not existing in fact.

2. Hurston's work is thus interestingly related to that of Carlos Castaneda (1968, 1971, 1972). On the one hand, De Mille (1990) shows that Castaneda's alleged ethnographies of Yaqui Indians are actually "brilliant allegories" involving the ideas of Garfinkel (1967), Huxley (1954), and Wittgenstein (1960), among others. Nonetheless, even De Mille thinks Castaneda "was dealing with concepts at the heart of social science in a way that might bring progress all anthropologists would some day thank him for" (139). In contrast, Hurston's most prominent work is explicitly presented as a novel implicitly involving many of her ethnographic insights. However, Hurston's insight that people like Janie Crawford maintain their self-respect by embodying themselves in certain speech-acts is similar to one of Castaneda's concepts. "The path with heart was a metaphorical way of asserting that in spite of being impermanent one still had to proceed and had to be capable of finding satisfaction and personal fulfillment in the act of choosing the most amenable alternative and identifying oneself completely with it" (1968: 199).

3. Youtube1 is the Sky News version of the official video. Youtube2 is the CNN version of the unofficial video.

4. Kyerematen (1964) presents an image-proverb association that illustrates why this might occur. "A cockroach which has fallen among fowls. . . . Fowls will not spare a cockroach that falls in their midst. *He who falls victim to his enemies can expect little mercy*" (54). While this specific association derives from Ghana, it seems widely applicable throughout the world.

5. At the invitation of Du Bois, Nkrumah left his graduate studies in 1945 to help organize the fifth Pan-African Congress in Manchester. Joseph B. Danquah, among others, then persuaded Nkrumah to become secretary general of a Ghanaian political party advocating self-rule. He became prime minister in 1952, and president of his newly independent nation in 1957.

Together with editorial comments, English and Kalumba (1996: 253–292) present excerpts from Nkrumah's best-known book, *Consciencism* (1970), together with discussion by Hountondji (1983), his best-known critic. *Consciencism* culls from the history of Greek philosophy a hypothesis that metaphysical materialism is essentially a force for egalitarianism. Nkrumah recommends African socialists emphasize this hypothesis in advancing their ideology.

Works Cited

Adler, Stella. 1988. *The Technique of Acting.* N.Y.: Bantam Books.
Andrews, William L., Frances Smith Foster, and Trudier Harris. 1997. *The Oxford Companion to African American Literature.* N.Y.: Oxford University Press.
Aristotle. 1941. *Nicomachean Ethics.* Trans. by W. D. Ross in Richard McKeon, ed., *The Basic Works of Aristotle.* N.Y.: Random House.
Austin, J. L. 1962. *How to Do Things with Words.* Cambridge, Mass.: Harvard University Press.
Ba, Sylvia. 1973. *The Concept of Negritude in the Poetry of Leopold Sedar Senghor.* Princeton, N.J.: Princeton University Press.
Bach, Kent. 1973. *Exit-Existentialism.* Belmont, Calif.: Wadsworth Publishing Co., Inc.
———. 1998a. "Performatives." Edward Craig, ed., *Encyclopedia of Philosophy,* vol. 8. London: Routledge: 302–304.
———. 1998b. "Speech-Acts." Edward Craig, ed., *Encyclopedia of Philosophy,* vol. 9. London: Routledge: 81–87.
Bach, Kent and Robert M. Harnish. 1979. *Linguistic Communication and Speech Acts.* Cambridge: MIT Press.
———. 1992. "How Performatives Really Work." *Linguistics and Philosophy* 15: 93–110.
Batson, Susan 2007. *Truth.* N.Y.: Rugged Land, LLC.
Berger, Peter. 1990. "Sociological Perspectives—Society as Drama." D. Brissett and C. Edgley, eds., *Life as Theater,* 2nd edition. N.Y.: Aldine de Gruyter: 51–62. Reprinted from Peter L. Berger, ed., *Invitation to Sociology: A Humanistic Perspective.* N.Y.: Overlook Press: ix–xvii.
Boyd, Valerie. 2003. *Wrapped in Rainbows.* N.Y.: Scribner's.

Brando, Marlon. 1988. "Foreword" to Stella Adler, *The Technique of Acting*. N.Y.: Bantam Books: 1–2.

Browne, Ray B. and Pat Browne, eds. 2001. *The Guide to United States Popular Culture*. Madison: University of Wisconsin Press.

Brissett, D. and C. Edgley. 1990a. *Life as Theater*, 2nd edition. N.Y.: Aldine de Gruyter.

———. 1990b. "The Dramaturgical Perspective." D. Brissett and C. Edgley, eds., (1990a): 1–46.

Carby, Hazel V. 1991. "Foreword" to Zora Neale Hurston, *Seraph on the Suwanee*. N.Y.: Charles Scribner's Sons, 1948. Reprinted by HarperPerennial, N.Y.: vii–xviii.

Caine, Michael. 1997. *Acting in Film*. N.Y.: Applause Theatre Books.

Carmichael, Stokely with Michael Ekwueme Thelwell. 2003. *Ready for Revolution*. N.Y.: Scribner.

Castaneda, Carlos. 1968. *The Teachings of Don Juan: A Yaqui Way of Knowledge*. Los Angeles: University of California Press.

———. 1971. *A Separate Reality: Further Conversations with Don Juan*. N.Y.: Simon and Schuster.

———. 1972. *The Journey to Ixtlan: The Lessons of Don Juan*. N.Y.: Simon and Schuster.

Cesaire, Aime. 1939. *Return to My Native Land*. Reprinted by Penguin Books, N.Y.: 1969.

———. 1987. "What Is Negritude to Me," *Selected Proceedings of the First Conference of African Communities in the Americas: Miami*: 21–32. Reprinted in Carlos Moore, Tanya R. Saunders, and Shawna Moore, eds., *African Presence in the Americas* (Trenton, N.J.: African World Press, Inc., 1995): 13–19.

CNN. 2006. transcripts.cnn.com/TRANSCRIPTS/0612/31/sm.02.html. Retrieved 23 Feb. 2009.

Coburn, Randy Sue. 1984. "Interview with Jack Elliott." *Esquire* (April): 80–85.

Cunard, Nancy, ed. 1934. *Negro: An Anthology*. London: Wishart. Reprinted by Frederick Ungar, N.Y.: 1970.

Cole, Herbert and Doran Ross. 1977. *The Arts of Ghana*. Los Angeles: Museum of Cultural History.

Davis, W. A. 2002. *Meaning, Expression, and Thought*. Cambridge, Mass.: Cambridge University Press.

De Mille, Richard. 1990. *The Don Juan Papers*. Belmont, Calif.: Wadsworth.

Du Bois, W. E. B. (1903). *The Souls of Black Folk*. Reprinted by Bantam Classics, N.Y.: 1989.

Ducrot, Oswald and Tzvetan Todorov. 1979. *Encyclopedia Dictionary of the Sciences of Language*. Trans. by Catherine Porter. Baltimore: Johns Hopkins University Press.

Dylan, Bob. 1966. "Interview." *Playboy* 13, no. 2 (March).

Easty, Edward Dwight. 1981. *On Method Acting*. N.Y.: Ivy Books.

Elliott, Ramblin' Jack. 1974. "Interview." *Guitar Player* (Oct.): 6.
English, Parker. 1999. "Consciencism, Representative Realism, and Negritude." *African Philosophy* 12, no. 1 (March): 69–94.
English, Parker and Kibujjo M. Kalumba, eds. 1996. *African Philosophy: A Classical Approach.* Upper Saddle River, N.J.: Prentice Hall.
Fingarette, Herbert. 1967. "Performatives." *American Philosophical Quarterly* 4, no. 1 (January): 39–48.
———. 1972. *Confucius—The Secular as Sacred.* N.Y.: Harper Torchbooks. Reissued by Waveland Press, Inc.: 1998.
Fletcher, Juanita D. 1976. Letter to Ms. Michelle D. Kourouma of the Southern Conference of Black Mayors (February 3) from a "Specialist in Afro-American History and Culture at the Library of Congress." Maitland, Fla.: Public Library; VF Hurston, Zora Neale; ACC. NO. 6289.
Frankl, Victor. 1946. *Man's Search for Meaning.* Reprinted by Washington Square Press, N.Y.: 1985.
Garfinkel, Harold. 1967. *Studies in Ethnomethodology.* Englewood Cliffs, N.J.: Prentice Hall.
Gates, Henry Louis, Jr. 1988. *The Signifying Monkey.* N.Y.: Oxford University Press.
Ginsberg, Michel Peled. 1977. "Free Indirect Discourse: Theme and Narrative Voice in Flaubert, George Eliot, and Verga," Ph.D. dissertation. Yale University.
Goffman, Erving. 1959. *The Presentation of Self in Everyday Life.* N.Y.: Doubleday.
———. 1961. "Role Distance." *Encounters.* N.Y.: Bobbs-Merrill. Reprinted by D. Brissett and C. Edgley, eds., *Life as Theater,* 2nd edition. N.Y.: Aldine de Gruyter. 1990: 101–11.
———. 1986. *Frame Analysis: An Essay on the Organizing of Experience.* Boston: Northeastern University Press.
Grainger, Roger and Mary Duggan. 1997. *Imagination, Identification and Catharsis in Theatre and Therapy.* London: Jessica Kingsley Publishers.
Grice, H. P. 1957. "Meaning." *Philosophical Review* 66, no. 3 (July): 377–88.
Hagen, Uta. 1973. *Respect for Acting.* N.Y.: Macmillan.
———. 1991. *A Challenge for the Actor.* N.Y.: Macmillan.
Heidegger, Martin. 1927. *Being and Time.* Trans. by J. Macquarie and E. Robinson. Oxford: Basil Blackwell, 1973.
Hemenway, Robert E. 1977. *Zora Neale Hurston: A Literary Biography.* Urbana: University of Illinois Press. Reprinted by Illini Books, 1980.
Hentoff, Nat. 1963. Jacket notes for *The Freewhellin' Bob Dylan.* N.Y.: Columbia Records.
Hill, Lynda Marion. 1996. *Social Rituals and the Verbal Art of Zora Neale Hurston.* Washington, D.C.: Howard University Press.
Holloway, Karla F. C. 1987. *The Character of the Word.* N.Y.: Greenwood Press.
Holt, David. 1992. "Enactment, Therapy and Behaviour." S. Jennings, ed., *Dramatherapy: Theory and Practice 2.* London: Tavistock/Routledge: 68–81.

Horton, Robin. 1967. "African Traditional Thought and Western Science." *Africa* XXVII, nos. 1 and 2: 50–71, 155–87. Abridged and reprinted in English and Kalumba, eds. *African Philosophy: A Classical Approach*. Upper Saddle River, N.J.: Prentice Hall: 193–215.

Hough, Graham. 1970. "Narration and Dialogue in Jane Austen." *Critical Quarterly* XII.

Hountondji, Paulin J. 1983. *African Philosophy: Myth and Reality*. Bloomington: Indiana University Press.

Howard, Lillie P. 1987. "Zora Neale Hurston." Trudier Harris and Thadious M. Davis, eds., *Dictionary of Literary Biography*. Detroit: Gale Research Company: 133–45.

Hughes, Langston. 1926. "The Negro Artist and the Racial Mountain." *The Nation* (June): 692–94.

Hurston, Zora Neale. 1934a. "Characteristics of Negro Expression." Nancy Cunard, ed., *Negro: An Anthology*. London: Wishart. Reprinted by Frederick Ungar, N.Y.: 1970: 24–31.

———. 1934b. "Shouting." Cunard (1934/1970): 34–35.

———. 1935. *Mules and Men*. Philadelphia: J. B. Lippincott. Reprinted by Perennial Library, N.Y.: 1990.

———. 1937. *Their Eyes Were Watching God*. Philadelphia: J. B. Lippincott. Reprinted by Perennial Classics, N.Y.: 1998.

———. 1942. *Dust Tracks on a Road: An Autobiography*. Philadelphia: J. B. Lippincott. Reprinted by HarperPerennial, N.Y.: 1996.

———. 1948. *Seraph on the Suwanee*. N.Y.: Charles Scribner's Sons. Reprinted by HarperPerennial, N.Y.: 1991.

Huxley, Aldous. 1954. *The Doors of Perception*. N.Y.: Harper.

Irele, Abiola. 1986. "The Negritude Debate." Albert Bernard, ed., *European-Language Writing in Sub-Saharan Africa*, vol. 1. Budapest: Akademia Kiado.

James, William. 1896. "The Will to Believe." Reprinted in *The Will to Believe and Human Immortality*. N.Y.: Dover, 1960.

Johnson, J. R., Town Clerk. 1887. "Notice of Incorporation (August 15)." Uncited photocopy in the Public Library of Maitland, Florida (VF: Eatonville, Fla.; ACC. NO. 4948).

Kane, Robert. 1996. "Anselm's Modal Argument." Stephen H. Phillips, ed., *Philosophy of Religion*. Fort Worth, Tex.: Harcourt Brace College Publishers: 155–61.

Kazantzakis, Nikos. 1955. *The Last Temptation of Christ*. Trans. by Peter A. Bien. N.Y.: Scribner Paperback Fiction, 1988.

Kesteloot, Lilyan. 1974. *Black Writers in French: A Literary History of Negritude*. Translated by Ellen Conroy Kennedy. Philadelphia: Temple University Press.

Knobler, Peter. 1989. Liner notes to *Tom Rush: Blues, Songs and Ballads*. Berkeley, Calif.: Fantasy.

Kyerematen, A. A. Y. 1964. *The Panoply of Ghana*. N.Y.: Praeger.

Lahr, John. 2001. "The Alchemist." *The New Yorker* (October 15): 88–96.

Lane, Anthony. 1997. "Tough Guy and Nice Guy." *The New Yorker* (July 14): 31–32.
Lewis, Shireen K. 2006. "What Was Negritude?" *Race, Culture, and Identity*. N.Y.: Rowman and Littlefield: 23–54.
London, Justin. 2001. "Rhythm" in Stanley Sadie, ed., *The New Grove Dictionary of Music and Musicians* (N.Y.: Macmillan) 21: 277–309.
Lomax, Alan. 1960. "Zora Neale Hurston—A Life of Negro Folklore." *Sing Out!* 10 (Oct.–Nov.)
Loy, Hui-Chieh. 2002. "What Has J. L. Austin to Do with Confucius?" *International Philosophical Quarterly* 42, no. 2 (June): 193–208.
Magee, Bryan. 1999. "A Note on J. L. Austin and the Drama." *Philosophy* 74, no. 287: 119–21.
Mamet, David. 1999. *True and False*. N.Y.: Vintage Books.
Markovitz, Irving Leonard. 1969. *Leopold Sedar Senghor and the Politics of Negritude*. N.Y.: Atheneum.
Martin, Darnell, director. 2005. *Their Eyes Were Watching God*. Chicago: Harpo Studios.
Mbiti, John. 1969. *African Religions and Philosophy*. London: Heinemann. Reprinted in 1990. Excerpts reprinted in Parker English and Kibujjo M. Kalumba, eds. *African Philosophy: A Classical Approach*. Upper Saddle River, N.J.: Prentice Hall: 66–80.
McHale, Brian. 1978. "Free Indirect Discourse: A Survey of Recent Accounts." *PTL* 3: 249–87.
McLeod, M. D. 1981. *The Asante*. London: British Museums Publications.
Meisner, Sanford and Dennis Longwell. 1987. *Sanford Meisner on Acting*. N.Y.: Vintage Books.
Menil, Rene. 1941. "Orientation de la poesie." *Tropiques*, no. 2 (July).
Messinger, Sheldon L., Harold Sampson, and Robert D. Towne. 1962. "Life as Theater: Some Notes on the Dramaturgic Approach to Social Reality." *Sociometry* XXV (September): 98–110. Reprinted in D. Brissett and C. Edgley, eds. *Life as Theater*, 2nd edition. N.Y.: Aldine de Gruyter, 1990: 73–84.
Miller, T. G. 1984. "Goffman, Social Acting, and Moral Behavior." *Journal for the Theory of Social Behavior* 14, no. 2: 141–63.
Minh-Ha, Trinh. 1987. "Grandma's Story." Brian Wallis, ed., *Blasted Allegories*. N.Y.: New Museum of Contemporary Art: 2–32.
Nagel, Thomas. 1969. "Sexual Perversion." *Journal of Philosophy* 66, no. 1 (January): 5–17.
Nkrumah, Kwame. 1970. *Consciencism*. N.Y.: Monthly Review Press. Abridged and reprinted in English and Kalumba, eds. *African Philosophy: A Classical Approach*. Upper Saddle River, N.J.: Prentice Hall: 253–77.
North, Michael. 1994. "'Characteristics of Negro Expression': Zora Neale Hurston and the *Negro* Anthology." *The Dialect of Modernism*. N.Y.: Oxford. Reprinted 1998: 175–95.

Olivier, Laurence. 1982. *Confessions of an Actor*. Hammondsworth, England: Penguin Books.
———. 1986. *On Acting*. London: George Weidenfeld and Nicolson Ltd.
Omoregbe, J. I. 1981. "Two Ways of Looking at Death." *Nigerian Journal of Philosophy* 1, no. 1 (July): 31–39.
Pascal, Roy. 1977. *The Dual Voice: Free Indirect Discourse and Its Functioning in the Nineteenth-Century European Novel*. Totowa, N.J.: Rowman and Littlefield.
Plant, Deborah. 1995. *Every Tub Must Sit on Its Own Bottom: The Philosophy and Politics of Zora Neale Hurston*. Urbana: University of Illinois Press.
Preece, Harold. 1936. "The Negro Folk Cult." *Crisis* 43: 364, 374.
Prine, John. 2005. "Interview." *World Cafe* (National Public Radio: July 2).
Recanati, Francis. 1998. "Pragmatics." Edward Craig, ed., *Encyclopedia of Philosophy*, vol. 8. London: Routledge: 620–33.
Reed, John and Clive Wake. 1965. "Introduction." *Leopold Sedar Senghor: Prose and Poetry*. John Reed and Clive Wake, eds. and trans. Reprinted by Heinemann, London, 1979: 1–26.
Robinson, Lisa Clayton. 1999. "Hurston, Zora Neale." Kwame Anthony Appiah and Henry Louis Gates, Jr., eds., *Africana: The Encyclopedia of the African and African American Experience*. N.Y.: Basic Books: 981–83.
Ross, Doran. 1977. "The Iconography of Asante Sword Ornaments." *African Arts* 11, no. 1 (October): 16–25, 90–91.
Salamone, Debbie. 1988. "Black Town Challenges Eatonville." *Orlando Sentinel* (August 29): B-1.
Sartre, Jean Paul. 1939. "The Wall." Reprinted in Lloyd Alexander, ed. and trans., *Intimacy*. N.Y.: New Directions, 1975: 1–17.
———. 1943. *Being and Nothingness*. Trans. by Hazel E. Barnes. N.Y.: Philosophical Library, 1956.
———. 1948. "Black Orpheus." Introduction to Leopold Senghor, ed., *Anthology of the New Black and Malagasy Poetry in the French Language*. Paris: Presses Universitaires de France. Translated by S. W. Allen. Paris: Presence Africaine, 1963.
———. 1957. *Existentialism and Human Emotions*. Trans. by Hazel E. Barnes. Secaucus, N.J.: Citadel Press.
Searle, John R. 1969. *Speech Acts: An Essay in the Philosophy of Language*. Cambridge, Mass.: Cambridge University Press.
———. 1989. "How Performatives Work." *Linguistics and Philosophy* 12: 535–58.
Senghor, Leopold. 1948. *Anthology of the New Black and Malagasy Poetry in the French Language*. Paris: Presses Universitaires de France.
———. 1956. *Ethiopiques*. Paris: Seuil.
———. 1959. "The Psychology of the African Negro." *Presence Africaine*, Special Issue, 2nd Congress of Negro Writers and Artists. Reprinted in Albert H. Berrian and Richard A. Long, eds. *Negritude: Essays and Studies*. Hampton, Va.: Hampton Institute Press, 1967: 48–55.

———. 1963. "Negritude and African Socialism." Kenneth Kirkwood, ed., *African Affairs*. London: Chatto and Windus: 9–22.

———. 1965. *Leopold Sedar Senghor: Prose and Poetry* [from 1939 to 1962]. Edited and translated by John Reed and Clive Wake. London: Oxford University Press. Reprinted by Heinemann: London, 1979.

———. 1970. "Negritude: A Humanism of the Twentieth Century." Wilfred Cartey and Martin Kilson, eds. *The African Reader: Independent Africa*. N.Y.: Vintage Books: 179–92.

———. 1971. *The Foundations of "Africanite" or "Negritude" and "Arabite."* Trans. by Mercer Cook. Paris: Presence Africaine.

———. 1987. "Negritude and the Civilization of the Universal." *Selected Proceedings of the First Conference of African Communities in the Americas: Miami*: 21–32. Reprinted in Carlos Moore, Tanya R. Saunders, and Shawna Moore, eds., *African Presence in the Americas*. Trenton, N.J.: African World Press, Inc., 1995.

Siebel, Mark. 2003. "Illocutionary Acts and Attitude Expression." *Linguistics and Philosophy* 26: 351–66.

Simon, Paul. 1984. "Interview." *Playboy* 31, no. 2 (February): 49–55, 163–74.

Stanislavsky, Konstantin. 1924. *My Life in Art*. Trans. by Robert M. MacGregor. N.Y.: Theatre Arts Books, 1948.

———. 1936. *An Actor Prepares*. Trans. by Elizabeth Reynolds Hapgood. N.Y.: Theatre Arts Books, 1959.

———. 1949. *Building Character*. Trans. by Elizabeth Reynolds Hapgood. N.Y.: Theatre Arts Books, 1969.

Strasberg, Lee. 1987. *A Dream of Passion: The Development of the Method*. Boston: Little, Brown and Company.

Strawson, P. F. 1959. "Persons." *Individuals* (Methuen). Reprinted by Anchor Books, N.Y., 1963: 81–113.

———. 1964. "Intention and Convention in Speech-acts." *Philosophical Review* 74, no. 4: 439–60.

Streng, F. J. 1982. "Three Approaches to Authentic Existence: Christian, Confucian, and Buddhist." *Philosophy East and West* 32, no. 4 (October): 371–89.

Tempels, Placide. 1945. *Bantu Philosophy*. Translated and reprinted by Presence Africaine Editions, Paris: 1959. Abridged and reprinted in English and Kalumba, eds., *African Philosophy: A Classical Approach*. Upper Saddle River, N.J.: Prentice Hall: 18–39.

"Theism in Western Thought." 2004. *Encyclopædia Britannica*. Retrieved 12 November, 2008, from Encyclopædia Britannica Online. search.eb.com/eb/article?tocId=38235 (23 Feb. 2009).

Thomson, Carol A. 1995. "Catalogue." Allen F. Roberts, ed., *Animals in African Art*. N.Y.: Museum for African Art: 104–86.

Turner, Ralph. 1962. "Role-taking: Process versus Conformity." Arnold M. Rose, ed., *Human Behavior and Social Processes*. N.Y.: Houghton Mifflin Co. Reprinted by

D. Brissett and C. Edgley, eds., *Life as Theater*, 2nd edition. N.Y.: Aldine de Gruyter. 1990: 85–100.

Uchendu, V. C. 1956. *The Igbos of Southeast Nigeria.* N.Y.: Holt, Rinehart and Winston.

Ullmann, Stephen. 1957. *Style in the French Novel.* Cambridge, Mass.: Cambridge University Press.

Urmson, J. O. 1998. "Austin, John Langshaw." Edward Craig, ed., *Encyclopedia of Philosophy*, vol 1. London: Routledge: 571–74.

Walker, Alice. 1979. "Dedication." Alice Walker, ed., *I Love Myself When I Am Laughing . . . and Then Again When I Am Looking Mean and Impressive: A Zora Neale Hurston Reader.* Old Westbury, N.Y.: Feminist Press: 1–5.

Wall, Cheryl. 1997a. "Hurston, Zora Neale." William L. Andrews, Frances Smith Foster, and Trudier Harris, eds., *The Oxford Companion to African American Literature.* N.Y.: Oxford University Press: 376–78.

———. 1997b. *"Their Eyes Were Watching God."* William L. Andrews, Frances Smith Foster, and Trudier Harris, eds., *The Oxford Companion to African American Literature.* N.Y.: Oxford University Press: 724.

Washington, Mary Helen. 1998. "Foreword." Zora Neale Hurston, *Their Eyes Were Watching God.* Philadelphia: J. B. Lippincott, 1937. Reprinted by Perennial Classics, N.Y.: ix–xvii.

Wilder, Gary. 2002. *The French Imperial Nation-State: Negritude and Colonial Humanism between the Two World Wars.* Chicago: University of Chicago Press.

Wittgenstein, Ludwig. 1960. *Tractatus Logico-Philosophicus.* N.Y.: Humanities.

Yaryan, Bill. 1965. "Interview with Pete Seeger." *Sing Out* (Nov).

Youtube1. 2009. www.youtube.com/watch?v=XYXczlVlLyY&feature=PlayList&p=DC82F9A7450E707F&playnext=1&index=10 (23 Feb. 2009).

Youtube2. 2009. www.youtube.com/watch?v=AYTwSBndv34 (23 Feb. 2009).

Index

acting: on/offstage, 24–25, 73, 80, 113, 118; professional, 23–24, 71–72, 87, 118; speech in, 30–31; twentieth-century European, 69. *See also* Method acting
acts: illocutionary, 36, 56n1, 76, 82n7; locutionary, 56n1, 82n7; perlocutionary, 56n1, 74–76, 82n7
addressee, 35; illocutionary attitudes, recognizing, 53–54; uptake, 37
Adler, Stella, 23
African art, 19n7
African societies, 13
"Amos Hicks" (*Their Eyes Were Watching God*), 29
ancestors, 2, 12, 18n3
animism, 11–12, 18n2, 19n4, 31–32; for speech, relevance of, 22–23
Aristotle, 107
attitude, 4–5, 42, 117; act-embodied, 4; Grice on, 59n12; speech-embodied, 48
attitude, affective, 2, 21–22, 26, 31; professional acting and, 23–24; Senghor on, 12–13

attitude, illocutionary, 2, 32, 35–36, 55, 66–67, 72, 80, 101, 117; addressee recognition of, 53–54; associated with utterances, 45; communication and, 37; intentionalism and, 39; isolation and, 47–48; without reflexivity, 41
audience, in presentationalism, 84n12
Austin, J. L., 1–2, 34n8, 35, 40, 64, 100, 119; on conventionalism, 77–79; on emotion, 27; special theory v. general theory of, 82n7; speech-act theories, 6, 58n10

Ba, Sylvia, 10
Bach, Kent, 6, 54, 72, 84n15, 119; on communicative embodiment, 51; on communicative success, 39, 53, 55; on conventionalism, 77; on intentionalism, 36–37, 39, 60n16; objections to views of, 41–42; on performatives, 58n9; on reflexive intention, 37–38, 46; on superimpositions, 60n15
Batson, Susan, 75

131

Index

behavior, 63, 82–83n8; criteria, 83n10; patterns of, 63. *See also* social behavior
Binoche, Juliette, 75
Black(s): affective energy, 30; assimilation, 10; dialect, 87; emotions, 2; speech, 13–14
"Black Orpheus" (Sartre), 5–6
Brandon, Marlon, 33n2

Caine, Michael, 72, 103
Carmichael, Stokely, 57n3, 98
Castaneda, Carlos, 120n2
"Charlie" (*Their Eyes Were Watching God*), 44, 54
Christianity, 112
Collins, Judy, 105–6
communication, 37, 80; Method theory and, 24–25; speech as, 39
communicative embodiment, 51
communicative intention, 39, 42–43; elements of, 42; identifying, 39–41; individual, 50; Janie's, 45
communicative sincerity, 41
communicative success. *See* success, communicative
concentration, 24–25
Consciencism (Nkrumah), 121n5
convention(s): extralinguistic, 36, 48, 65; linguistic, 65, 81n1; social rituals and, 62–63
conventionalism, 35–36, 61, 65, 82n4, 83n10, 117; about performatives, 56; criticisms of, 77–79; v. intentionalism, 37, 46–48, 55, 59n10, 67–69; interpretations within, 79–81, 116; on performatives, 63–64; self-awareness and, 47–48; speech, 55
cultural generalization, 7–8n3

Davis, W. A., 37
death: Dylan on, 7n1; optimistic v. pessimistic views of, 3–5; optimistic view of, 7n2; speech-acts before, 3–5, 112–16
declarations, 81n2, 82n5, 101, 109n13, 115; of God, 62; Hurston on, 59n13; from performatives, 56–57n2, 82n5; role and, 76–77
de Mille, Richard, 120n2
dialect, 87, 89–90
diction, 89–90, 92–93
discourse, 94; direct, 88, 90; indirect, 89–91; represented, 88
discourse, free indirect, 87–89; flaws in Gate's argument on, 91–95
discursive reason, 10
double-consciousness, 28, 81, 89–93, 99, 100
double-descriptives, 14
drama, 13–15, 20nn8–9; Senghor on, 12
dramaturgical concepts, 15–16, 31, 60n16; Negro expression and, 20n9
Du Bois, W. E. B., 1, 28, 81, 90–91, 95, 108n4, 121n5
Dylan, Bob, 34n7, 84n13, 100, 105; on death, 7n1; on expression of self, 4–5

Eatonville, 107–8n1, 112
effective action, 64
effects, perlocutionary, 40
Elliott, Ramblin' Jack, 84n13, 105–6, 110n20
emotion(s), 26–27, 80; amplification of, 13; Blacks v. White, 2. *See also* memory, emotional
energy, affective, 21–22, 25–28, 68, 117–18; animism and, 22; internalistically/externalistically used, 80; Janie's access to internalistic, 28, 100–102; misuses of, 28–29; performism and, 30–31; representationalism and, 102–7; Senghor on, 12–13; speaking with, 70–71; White v. Black, 30

externalism, 16, 55–56, 80; sense of self and, 95–97

Fingarette, Herbert, 61, 67, 72–75, 81n1, 83n9, 85n18, 119; on conventionalism, 77, 82n4; on effortlessness, 76; on magic, 63
folklore, ethnographic, 6, 13
folk music, 107
force: locutionary, 34n8; perlocutionary, 41, 117
force, illocutionary, 34n8, 38, 41, 46, 67, 82n5, 117; identification of, 80; role-expression and, 76
Frankl, Victor, 4
freedom: physical, 43; spiritual, 4, 43

Gates, Henry Louis, Jr., 1, 81, 87, 108nn4–5; argument as flawed, 91–95
God, 62
Goffman, Erving, 15–16; role distance, concept of, 43
Grice, H. P., 37–38, 74; on attitude, 59n12; on reflexivity and sex, 51; speech-act theories, 58n10
Guthrie, Woody, 84n13, 106

Hagen, Uta, 69, 84n11; on affective attitude, 23, 26
Hale, Nathan, 113
Harnish, Robert M., 6, 54, 84n15, 119; on communicative embodiment, 51; on communicative success, 39, 53, 55; on intentionalism, 36–37, 39, 60n16; objections to views of, 41–42; on performatives, 58n9; on reflexive intention, 37–38, 46
Heidegger, Martin, 3
Hemenway, Robert E., 15, 28, 108–9n8, 109n14; on Hurston, 20n11, 21, 32–33n1
hieroglyphics, 14–15, 17
Hill, Joe, 113

Hill, Lynda Marion, 31; on performism, 6, 15
Holloway, Karla F. C., 17
Holt, David, 24
Horton, Robin, 11–12
Howard, Lillie P., 58n7
Hughes, Langston, 100
Hurston, Zora Neale, 1, 29, 33–34n6, 44, 54, 72, 87–89, 94, 109n11, 112, 120n2; on affective energy, 28; on animism, 22–23; background for, 7–8n3, 13; as criticized, 30; on declarations, 59n13; on dramatic speech, 14–15; Harlem intellectuals, compared to, 32–33n1; on images and drama in speech, 13–15, 24; on John, 57n3; Negro expression, view of, 17, 20n11, 116–17; on particularization, 24; Plant on, 40; on rhythm within Negro expression, 16–17; on role-enactments, 16; Senghor's views related to, 1–2, 21–23; use of natural, 108–9n8
Hussein, Saddam, 114–15

Igbo, 49–50, 54
image(s), 31, 32; African, 10; Method theorists on, 24; multiplicity in meanings of, 18n1; in speech, 12–15
imitation, 104, 106–7
inner growth, 29
intention, 41, 50, 117. *See also* communicative intention; reflexive intentions
intentionalism, 55, 58n10, 83n10, 117; Bach and Harnish on, 36–37, 39, 60n16; v. conventionalism, 37, 46–48, 55, 59n10, 67–69; difficulties in describing, 37–39; interpretations within, 45–46, 79–81, 115–16; Janie exemplifying, 44; performatives and, 56, 65–66; self-awareness and, 47–48; speech-act within, 48–49, 55

134 ~ Index

intentionalistic success. *See* success, intentionalistic
internalism, 16, 55, 80, 100–102; interpretation within, 16; sense of self and, 95–97
interpretation: within conventionalism, 79–81, 116; within intentionalism, 45–46, 79–81, 115–16; within internalism/externalism, 16; listener, 17, 27, 36, 104
intuitive reason, 10

James, William, 84–85n16
"Janie Crawford" (*Their Eyes Were Watching God*), 1, 32, 33–34n6, 44–47, 54, 59–60n14, 67–68, 70–71, 102–3, 115, 120n2; affective energy exemplified by, 28, 100–102; attractiveness of, 109nn16–17; consciousness of, 108n5; dialect and diction of, 89–90; discourse associated with, 94; double-consciousness of, 90–91; Howard on, 58n7; reflexive mutual recognition and, 52–53; sense of self before becoming a woman, changes in, 95–97; sense of self of, evolution in, 87–88, 95–100, 102, 107; speech and sense of self with Joe, change in, 97–100, 102
"Joe Starks" (*Their Eyes Were Watching God*), 45, 88, 97–100, 102; free indirect discourse associated with, 93
"John" (*Mules and Men*), 40, 88; communicative intentions, 41–42; Hurston on, 57n3; linguistic performatives used by, 43–44; speech-acts of, 42–44; use of affective energy, 71

Kane, Robert, 112; on modal reformulation of Anselm's argument, 119–20n1
Kazantzakis, Nikos, 111

Knobler, Peter, 106–107
Kyerematen, A. A. Y., 121n4

Lane, Anthony, 103
languages, African, 10–12
The Last Temptation of Christ (Kazantzakis), 111
Lear, 69
"Lee Coker" (*Their Eyes Were Watching God*), 29
li, 63
life-force, 12, 18nn3–4, 22, 32
Lin, Carol, 114–15
listener(s): interpretations, 17, 27, 36, 104; responses, 48
listener-uptake, 45; absence of, 48–49; performative success and, 46–47
"Logan Killicks" (*Their Eyes Were Watching God*), 96–97
Lomax, Alan, 13
Loy, Hui-Chieh, 85n17
loyalty, reciprocal, 74–75, 80, 84–85n6

Magee, Bryan, 87
magic, 63, 82n5; Confucian, 61–63; defined, 63; natural, 75–76; supernatural, 62, 81n3
Mamet, David, 31; on concentration techniques, 25; on representationalism, 73; on speech, 26–27
Mbiti, John, 112
Meisner, Sanford, 69
memory, emotional, 23, 25
Messinger, Sheldon L., 34n7
metaphor, 14, 30
Method acting, 23–25, 31, 33n2, 72, 84n11
Mitchell, Burroughs, 30
Mules and Men (Hurston), 13

Nagel, Thomas, 6, 59n12, 101, 119; on communicative success, 50–53;

on reflexive mutual recognition, superimposed, 80; on sense of self, 74
"Nany" (*Their Eyes Were Watching God*), 95–96
negritude, 7, 100; Negro expression, as overlapping with, 1–2, 21–22; performism compared to, 31–32; Senghor on, background for, 9–10; Senghor's view of, 11–13, 19n6, 112, 116–17; subjective v. objective, 10–13, 18n2; Western-focused factors, 18n2
Negro culture, 58n6
Negro expression, 7, 57n3; dramaturgic concepts and, 20n9; Hurston view of, 17, 20n11, 116–17; negritude, as overlapping with, 1–2, 21–22; performism compared to, 31–32; rhythm within, 16–17
Negro performance, 16
Nigerian culture, 3, 49–50
Nigerian political prisoners, 113–16; speech-acts of, 118–19
Nkrumah, Kwame, 119, 121n5
North, Michael, 6, 31

oath, 49–50
"Ole Massa" (*Mules and Men*), 40, 57n3, 71; identifying John's communicative intentions, 41–42
Oliver, Laurence, 20n8, 33n2, 69, 84n14
Omoregbe, J. I., 3, 7n2
oral tradition, 11, 13–14, 18n2; Senghor's views on, 51
Orphic myth, 33

"Pablo" ("The Wall"), 4
particularization, 24
performance: implicit v. explicit, 64; magical, 63. *See also* Negro performance; social performance

performatives, 58n9, 82n7; declarations from, 56–57n2, 82n5; as effortless, 63–66; explicit, 83nn9–10; implicit, 67–68, 83n9; intentionalism v. conventionalism and, 56; playful, 43–44; Strawson on, 47
performatives, linguistic, 36, 57–58n4; explicit, 55; expressing submission, 40; success of, 37; used by John, 43–44
performative success. *See* success, performative
performism, 1, 6–7, 15, 29–30, 35, 55, 118; affective energy and, 30–31; as different from negritude and Negro expression, 31–32; presentationalism, related to, 68–70; race and, 114
Placide Tempels, 19n4
Plant, Deborah, 31, 109n14; on Hurston, 40; on performism, 6; on power of speech, 15
P-predicates, 79, 82–83n8, 83n10
Preece, Harold, 58n6
preliminary faith, concept of, 84–85n16
presentationalism, 69, 70–71, 80, 84n11, 84n14; audience and, 84n12; performism, related to, 68–70
Prine, John, 43
psychic satisfaction, 15, 21
Punter, Percival McGuire, 33–34n6, 59n13

racial discrimination, 2, 18n2
reasoning, intuitive, 13, 18n2
reflexive intentions, 6, 37–38, 46, 58–59n10; Siebel on, 59n11; Strawson on, 38
reflexive mutual recognition, 51; superimposed, 54–55, 74, 80; Tea Cake and, 52–53
reflexivity, 41, 46–47, 50–51
representationalism, 69, 71, 73, 84n11, 107; affective energy and, 102–7; speech-acts in, 72

respect, 72–74; reciprocal loyalty and, 74–75, 80, 84–85n6. *See also* self-respect
rhythm(s), 13, 70, 106; life-force, to awaken, 22; within Negro expression, 16–17; Senghor on, 12–13, 19n5
role(s), 76–77, 85n18, 96, 103; declarations and, 76–77; distance, 43; as patterns of behavior, 63
role-enactment(s), 56, 107; dramaturgical concepts of, 15; interpretations of, 55; self-awareness and, 15–16; Turner on, 29
role-expression, illocutionary force, 76
role-making, 20n9
role-management, 16
role-play, 55

Salamone, Debbie, 108n1
Sartre, Jean Paul, 4–6, 33n5; on affective attitude, 2; on optimistic view of death, 7n2; on subjective v. objective negritude, 11
Searle, John R., 81n1, 83n9, 119; on communicative success, 81n2; on conventionalism, 35–36, 77; on declarations from performatives, 56–57n2, 82n5; speech-act theories, 58n10; on supernatural magic, 62
self, sense of, 80; affective energy and, 71; embodied in speech-acts, 113–15; externalistic v. internalistic, 95–97; Janie's evolution of, 87–88, 95–100, 102, 107; Nagel on, 74; race-based, 100; speech-embodied, 46, 71–74, 87, 94, 116
self-awareness, 2–5, 55–56, 70; conscious speech and, 5–6; conventionalism v. intentionalism and, 47–48; hieroglyphics and, 15; role-enactments and, 15–16; speech to enhance, 6, 26–28, 32, 42–43; subjective negritude and, 13
self-control, 89–91

self-definition, 29
self-discipline, 72
self-identification, 66
self-respect, 100–102, 109n13, 120n2
Senghor, Leopold, 1; on animism, 22–23; background for, 9–10; as criticized, 30; Hurston's views related to, 1–2, 21–23; on intuitive reason, 10; on life-forces within animism, 19n4; negritude, view of, 11–13, 19n6, 112, 116–17; oral tradition, views on, 51; on particularization, 24; on rhythm, 12–13, 19n5; on speech, 70
Siebel, Mark, 37–38, 84n15; on reflexive intentions, 59n11
simile, 14, 30
Simon, Paul, 111
social behavior, 63, 74
social performance, 30, 43
social ritual: conforming to conventions within, 62–63; initial gesture in, 65, 72; participation in, 66–67
soul, 109n14; development of, 53; speech involving, 21
speakers, 21–22, 117
speech, 2, 5–6, 21, 38, 47, 55, 61; with affective energy, 70–71; animism for, relevance of, 22–23; bequesting, 47, 49; Black, 13–14; change in Janie's, 97–100, 102; as communication, 39; conventionalistic, 55; death, before, 3–5; dramatic, 14–15; effortlessness in, 66; as embodying sense of self, 46, 71–74, 87, 94, 116; exchange of, as relatively effortless, 74–77; image within, 12–15; Mamet on, 26–27; natural magic within, 75–76; Negro, 17; power of, 11–12, 15; in professional acting, 30–31; self-awareness, to enhance, 6, 27–28, 32, 42–43; Senghor on, 70; as social performance, 43; value of, 33n4; will to adorn, 14

speech-act(s), 111; angular form of, 104; as coming from the heart, 73–74; consequences of, 67–68; death, before imminently inevitable, 3–5, 112–16; effortlessness of, 76; Hussein's, 114–15; illocutionary, 6, 31; individual, 76–77; within intentionalism, 48–49, 55; interpretations of, 79–81; of Janie as Joe's wife, 98; of John, 42–44; of Nigerian political prisoners, 118–19; performative, 48; within presentationalism, 70; within representationalism, 72; sense of self embodied in, 113–15; theories, 6, 58n10
Stanislavsky, Konstantin, 69, 72–73
Strasberg, Lee, 23–24, 69, 101
Strawson, P. F., 82–83n8, 99; on conventionalism, 65, 78–79; on intentions, 38; on linguistic/extralinguistic distinctions, 48; on performatives, 47; on P-predicates, 83n10; speech-act theories, 58n10
submission, 40, 42, 57–58n4, 71
success: illocutionary, 66, 74–75, 80; intentionalistic, 53–54; locutionary, 65–66
success, communicative, 39–41, 66, 81n2, 118; Bach and Harnish on, 39, 53, 55; Charlie and, 54; Nagel's view of, 50–53; requirements for, 49
success, performative, 45–47, 55; listener-uptake and, 46–47; v. statemental success, 48, 67
success, perlocutionary, 74–75; intentionalistic success, associated with, 53–54

success, statemental, 45, 55; conventionalism v. intentionalism and, 46–47; v. performative success, 48, 67
symbolism, Akan, 18n1
symmetry, 16

"Tea Cake Woods" (*Their Eyes Were Watching God*), 33–34n6, 44–45, 54, 59–60n14, 67–68, 70–71, 94, 103, 115; angular form of speech-acts, 104; compared with Collins, 105; features of, 110n18; reflexive mutual recognition and, 52–53
theater, 20n9
Their Eyes Were Watching God (Hurston), 1, 13, 29, 33–34n6, 44, 72, 94; discourse in, 87–89
Thompson, Carol A., 18n1
tone, 70, 106
transformation, extralinguistic, 62
transparent living, 50, 54
tropes, 32
Turner, Ralph, 63, 76; dramaturgical concept, 15–16; on role-enactments, 29
"Two Ways of Looking at Death" (Omoregbe), 3

Uchendu, V. C., 49–50, 54

verbs: in hieroglyphics, 14; performative, 66

"The Wall" (Sartre), 4
Wall, Cheryl, 13, 103, 108n6
Washington, Mary Helen, 103

About the Author

After serving as an Air Strike Control Officer in the Marines, **Parker English** earned his philosophy Ph.D. in 1974 from the University of Western Ontario. He next worked as a tree feller in northern Ontario, and later built a log cabin outside Goderich, Ontario. Between 1983 and 1987, English taught philosophy at the University of Calabar, Nigeria. He has published two dozen articles and book chapters, roughly half of which concern issues in African philosophy, and co-edited *African Philosophy: A Classical Approach* (Prentice-Hall). Summers, he enjoys bicycling; winters, for the sake of an aging body, he tolerates jogging.

Breinigsville, PA USA
05 August 2010
243040BV00004B/4/P